Fiona McDonald

studied classical painting and drawing at The Julian Ashton Art School in Sydney, Australia from 1985 to 1989. After moving to the Blue Mountains, she began developing her unique oil-painted, needle-sculpted, life-size cloth figures, and her own line of fabric dolls and dragons. On returning to her home town of Armidale, Fiona added to her skills by learning to knit. This latest phase in her career has resulted in her developing designs for dolls and other toys.

Knitted Fairies

to Cherish and Charm

Dedication

This book is for Isabelle Beatriz,
who believes in fairies.

Knitted Fairies
to Cherish and Charm

Fiona McDonald

Search Press

First published in Great Britain 2011

Search Press Limited
Wellwood, North Farm Road,
Tunbridge Wells, Kent TN2 3DR

Text copyright © Fiona McDonald 2011

Photographs by Paul Bricknell at Search Press Photographic Studio

Photographs and design copyright © Search Press Ltd. 2011

ISBN: 978-1-84448-360-0

The Publishers and author can accept no responsibility for any
consequences arising from the information, advice or instructions given
in this publication.

Suppliers
If you have difficulty in obtaining any of the materials and equipment
mentioned in this book, then please visit the Search Press website for
details of suppliers: www.searchpress.com

Printed in China

Acknowledgements

All my thanks to the Search Press team,
especially Roz Dace and Katie Sparkes;
thanks to my agent Isabel Atherton
of Creative Authors and to
Australian Country Spinners for
their huge supply of Cleckheaton Country
8-ply yarn, which forms the basis of
nearly all my knitting.

ABBREVIATIONS

K	knit
P	purl
K2tog	knit two together
P2tog	purl two together
inc	increase by knitting into the same stitch twice
rem	remain
SS	stocking stitch
GS	garter stitch

Contents

Introduction

"When the first baby laughed for the first time, his laugh broke into a million pieces, and they all went skipping about. That was the beginning of fairies."

(Peter Pan in Kensington Gardens by J. M. Barrie)

Peter Pan also tells us that "every time a child says 'I don't believe in fairies', there is a fairy somewhere that falls down dead".

Well, I hope you do believe in fairies because I do: and to prove it I have designed ten different fairies based on my observations in the field, or rather the bottom of my overgrown garden. Fairies all have their own special magic powers: some good, some bad and some a little of both. They often reflect the natural world around them, such as tree-dwelling fairies, flower fairies and water fairies, or the changing seasons, such as the snow fairy and the autumn fairy. Every place in the world has its own fairies. Why not take a sketchbook and find a quiet corner at home or in the garden to sit for an hour or so to watch for fairies. Take notes and make sketches, then, inspired by your flights of fancy into the fairy realm, create your own knitted fairies based on the patterns in this book. Above all else, have fun, enjoy making these wonderful little beings, and add a touch of magic to your home.

Knitting fairies for very young children

Some of the fairy dolls in this book have wired wings and small items of beaded jewellery that should not be included if you intend to give your fairy to a small child to play with. Simply make sure there are no small parts that could be chewed, pulled or sucked off and swallowed, and no sharp wires that could scratch or damage the skin or eyes, and all of the fairy dolls will make beautiful gifts for children of all ages. For the neck of the doll, I would either not use any stiffening at all, or only use cardboard.

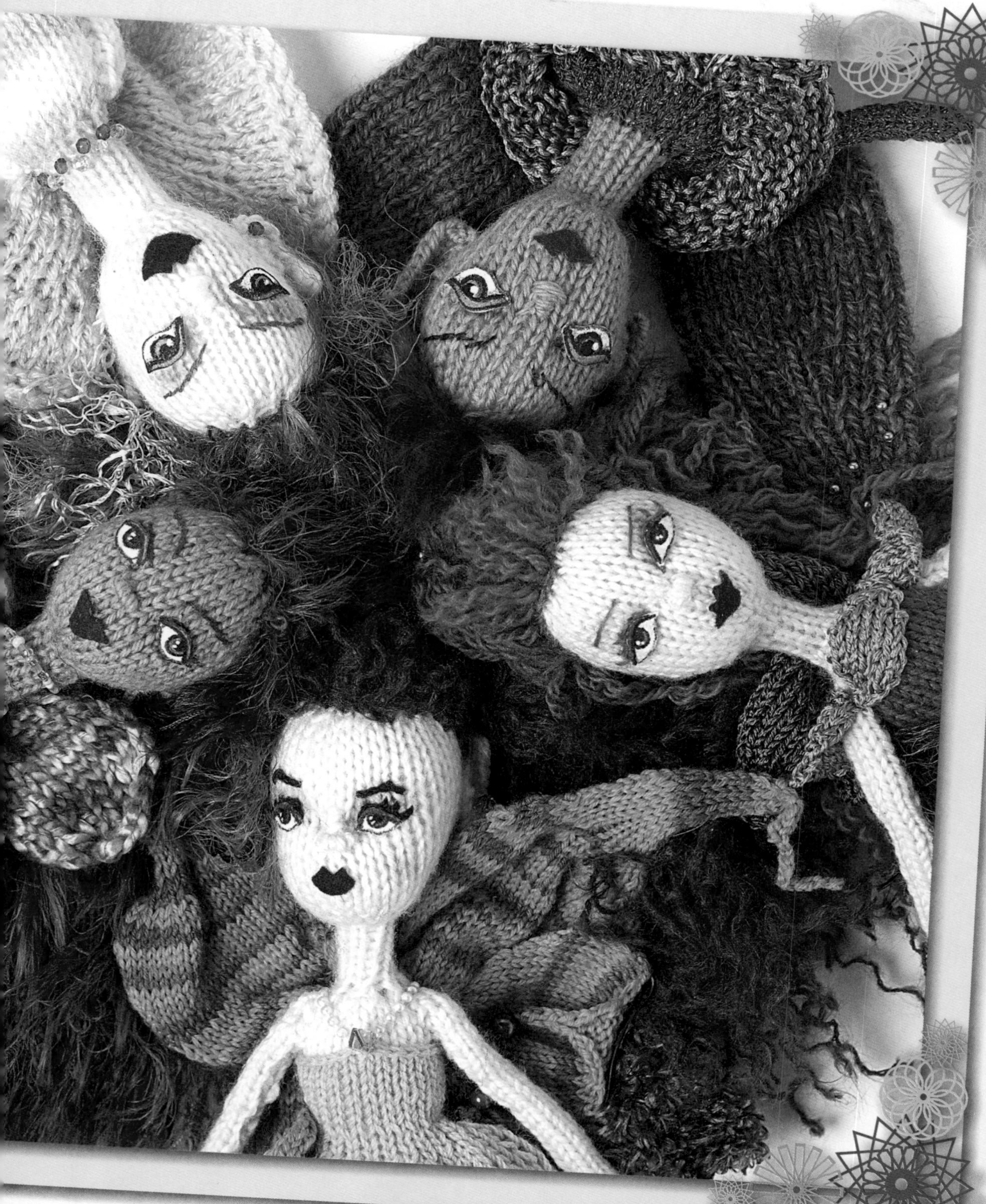

Materials and techniques

Yarns and embellishments

There are no hard-and-fast rules about knitting up these fairies. You can use oddments of yarn, ribbons, buttons, beads and wires that you may have stashed away at home, or you can use any of the beautiful yarns and embellishments that are available in shops and on the internet. Of course, the closer you can match the yarn weight and needle size I have used the better. I have knitted the bodies, arms and legs in a double-knitting yarn (also known as 8-ply or light worsted), and used 3mm (US 3) needles. For the clothes I have used 7mm (US 11) and 4mm (US 6). The firmer the knitting on the doll's body, the better shape it will be and less stretch will occur.

Stuffing

I use polyester fibrefill for the stuffing. This is the type of stuffing used to fill cheap pillows, which may well be the most economical way of obtaining it, or it can be purchased as toy stuffing. I use an old paintbrush with the bristles still attached for poking stuffing into bodies and legs. The bristles help hold the stuffing as you push it downwards. You will notice that I have not stuffed the legs of any of the female fairies – this gives them a slender, ethereal appearance. I also have not stuffed any of the arms. The male fairies' legs are all stuffed carefully – avoid over-stuffing them, otherwise they will look too large and out of proportion to the rest of their bodies.

When stuffing your doll, use smallish pieces so that you don't get big, misshapen lumps where you don't want them. Massage the stuffing into place, and avoid over-stuffing. As a general rule, try not to put so much stuffing in that the knitting stretches apart.

Supporting the neck

Because of their slender necks, these fairies require some kind of armature that acts as a backbone through the body and into the head. You can use a thin roll of cardboard, an unsharpened pencil, a chopstick or a length of dowelling bound tightly with tape. These need to be fine enough to go into the neck without making it bulge. I like to wrap sticky tape around the backbone, twisting it so that the sticky side is on the outside. I then wrap a fine layer of stuffing around it before inserting it up through the body and neck and into the head. Remember to put a little stuffing in the head first.

Checklist

For knitting the fairies:

* Double-knitting yarn (8-ply/light worsted) for the fairy bodies
* 3mm (US 3) knitting needles

For making the bodies:

* Polyester fibrefill
* Old paintbrush
* Cardboard, pencil, chopstick or dowelling to support the neck
* Sticky tape
* Tapestry needle for needlesculpting

For the faces:

* White and lip-coloured felt
* Quick-drying craft glue
* Acrylic paints and/or fine felt-tip pens
* Coloured pencils (optional)
* Very fine paintbrush
* Embroidery thread
* Eyelash yarn for eyelashes (optional)
* 2B pencil or air-soluble pen

For the wings, clothes and hair:

* Oddments of yarn in a variety of colours and types
* 7mm (US 11) and 4mm (US 6) knitting needles
* Fine floristry wire or chenille sticks
* Press-stud for attaching the wings to the fairy (optional)
* Sewing thread and needle
* Crochet hook

For finishing the fairies:

* Sewing thread, press-studs, floristry wire, chenille sticks, ribbons, beads, trimmings, silk flowers, etc.

Wiring the wings

To shape and stiffen the wings I have used fine floristry wire, mattress stitched in place around the edges of the wings using sewing thread. Ensure the ends of the wires are folded over and stitched firmly in place to avoid injury. If your fairy is intended for very small children, it is better not to wire the wings at all, as the sharp ends could work loose and harm the child.

Needlesculpting the body

If you want your fairy to have a more shapely body then try some needlesculpting. Thread a tapestry needle with the same yarn you used for the body. Push the needle into the torso and pull it out between the legs. Make a small securing stitch. Push the needle back into the torso close to this stitch and pull it out roughly where the belly button would be. Make another small stitch and push the needle back through the body and straight out the back. Make a line of small running stitches around the waist, starting and finishing at the back. Pull the thread gently until a shapely waist is achieved. Tie the loose threads together then neaten and trim.

   To shape the buttocks, take the thread down to between the legs and push the needle back into the body. There will be a long stitch going straight down from the lower back to the base of the body. Bring the yarn out through the back again, in the same position as it went in. Pull the yarn firmly and the stitch will pull the two buttocks into shape. Secure the thread with a tiny stitch, neaten and cut the thread.

Needlesculpting the head

To define the head, make a line of running stitches around the jawline, from the back of the head, around the front to the centre point under the chin, and back round the other side of the head to where you started. Pull the thread firmly, tie the two ends in a knot to secure, then neaten the loose threads before cutting the yarn. Note that the back of the head, at the base of the skull, is higher than the front of the neck beneath the chin. Your stitching therefore needs to be higher at the back than the front, and come round the neck on a slight diagonal.

Needlesculpting the face

By sculpting the face you can obtain a more realistic shape.

1. Take a tapestry needle and a length of flesh-coloured yarn. Push the needle in through the back of the head or neck and pull it out to one side of where the top of the nose will be. Make a small securing stitch and push the needle back through the head. Pull the thread firmly but not too hard. This will form the inner corner of one eye socket; repeat on the other side of the face for the inner corner of the other eye socket.

2. Now push the needle and thread back into the doll from the back of the head and come out 1cm (½in) to the side of the inner corner of the eye to form the outer corner. Pull the thread firmly, make a small stitch and push the needle through the head to come out at the inner corner of the eye again. Make another small stitch and take the thread under the nose to come out at the inner corner of the other eye. Pull the thread firmly, make a small stitch and come out at the outer corner of the eye. Make a small stitch and push the needle back through the head. Pull the thread firmly without distorting the face too much. When you are happy with the shape of your fairy's face, secure with a stitch and neaten the thread.

Nose

Embroider the nose by taking a length of flesh-coloured yarn. Push the needle in through the back of head and come out where you wish the tip of the nose to be. Make two parallel and partly overlapping stitches across one or two knitted stitches to form the end of the nose. For a cute little nose, there is no need to make any more stitches. If you want a larger or more mature nose, continue to make stitches up the bridge of the nose towards the forehead.

Making the eyes and mouth

For the eyes and mouth you will need small pieces of white and lip-coloured felt, quick-drying craft glue, acrylic paints and/or fine felt-tip pens. If using paints, you will also need very fine-tipped paintbrushes (the type used for painting models). The eyebrows are embroidered on using embroidery thread of varying thicknesses.

1. Trace the templates of your choice. Cut them out and draw around them on to the felt.
2. Following the template, draw the pupil, iris and eyelid on to each eye, then colour in the iris and the eyelid using either acrylic paints or felt-tip pens. When dry, put in the pupil and paint or draw on a brown line to look like the eyelashes on the top lid.
3. Finish each eye with a dot or two of white paint to make it look shiny. This will really bring your doll's face to life.
4. Use craft glue to glue on each eye between the inner and outer corners of the eye socket. Attach the mouth just below the nose. Position the features carefully and make sure you are happy with your fairy's appearance before gluing in place.

Eyebrows

These are embroidered on using straight stitches worked in stranded embroidery thread. Varying the shape and thickness of the eyebrows can alter the character of your fairy dramatically. Try sketching different eyebrow shapes on to a drawn face first to decide what kind of expression you wish to achieve, then draw them on to your doll using a sharp 2B pencil or an air-soluble pen.

Templates

These templates are shown actual size, so there is no need to enlarge or reduce them. The colours are for guidance only – feel free to colour your fairy's eyes and lips exactly as you wish.

Eyelashes

Eyelashes are optional, and are really only necessary on female fairies. For realistic eyelashes, such as those on Alexis the Ice Fairy and Rainbow Dream Fairy, cut 1cm (½in) of eyelash yarn. Trim it diagonally so that the lashes taper, fit them to the eyelid and trim to size. Glue on the eyelashes with craft glue. Alternatively, embroider on the eyelashes using the same thread as you used for the eyebrows, as for Titania the Fairy Queen.

Colouring the face

You may want to shade the face for extra depth and character. Use very watery acrylic paint applied with a fine-tipped brush, or finely sharpened coloured pencils. Apply thin paint or pencil to the eyelid/socket area as you would makeup (you might prefer to do this before gluing on the eyes). Dab a little colour on to the cheeks if you wish. Dab excess colour off with a tissue.

Hair

This is where you can really let your imagination run wild! It is also a great opportunity to try out some of the amazing fancy, decorative and specialist yarns that are available.

I use several techniques for attaching hair, but my favourite is the rooted method, as the result looks as if it is growing out of the fairy's head.

Rooted hair

1. Find a book or DVD case that is the same height as the length of hair you want. Wind the yarn around it lengthways, not too tightly, and cut through the loops along one side, then separate the threads. Each thread will form two strands of hair.
2. Take a strand of yarn and fold it in half. Insert a crochet hook under a knitted stitch on the fairy's scalp, and use it to pull the yarn through the stitch to form a loop.
3. Pass the two ends of the yarn through the loop and pull it tight to make a knot.
4. Repeat until the head is covered in fabulous hair.

Glued hair

You can glue hair on to the fairy's head, especially if it is short and fluffy, but be careful not to get into a gluey mess. Try small sections first.

Stitched hair

Cobweb the Dark Fairy has a large, loose bun on her head made by winding yarn around five fingers of one hand. When enough yarn is wound on to the fingers, snip the yarn from the ball. Slip the wound yarn from your fingers and position it on the fairy's head. Pin it down and then stitch it firmly in place all round with either sewing thread or yarn of the same colour.

For her long pony tail, wind some yarn around a book or DVD case, as above. Cut through the loops along one end. Keep the lengths of yarn folded in half and stitch the bundle of threads through the middle of bun and on to the scalp to secure.

Basic fairy body

All of the fairies have the same basic body; only the legs and the colours used vary. The body and head are knitted as an all-in-one piece and require just one seam up the back. You will need about 50g (1¾oz) of double-knitting (DK) yarn, also known as 8-ply or light worsted, and a pair of 3mm (US 3) needles.

Torso and head

Cast on 24 sts.
rows 1–10: SS, ending with a purl row.

Waist

row 11: K2tog, K5, K2tog, K6, K2tog, K5, K2tog [20 sts].
rows 12–14: SS for 3 rows, starting with a purl row.
row 15: inc 1 st, K5, inc 1 st, K6, inc 1 st, K5, inc 1 st [24 sts].
rows 16–22: SS for 7 rows, starting with a purl row.

Shoulders

row 23: K6, inc 2 sts, K8, inc 2 sts, K6 [28 sts].
row 24: purl.
row 25: K6, K2tog twice, K8, K2tog twice, K6 [24 sts].
row 26: P2tog to end of row [12 sts].
row 27: K2tog, knit to last 2 sts, K2tog [10 sts].

Neck

rows 28–34: SS for 7 rows.

Head

row 35: knit, inc 1 st at each end [12 sts].
row 36: purl, inc 1 st at each end [14 sts].
row 37: K6, inc 2 sts, K6 [16 sts].
row 38: purl.
row 39: inc 3 sts, K3, inc 4 sts, K3, inc 3 sts [26 sts].
row 40: purl.
row 41: knit, inc 1 st at each end [28 sts].
row 42: purl.
row 43: knit, inc 1 st at each end [30 sts].

rows 44–56: SS for 13 rows.
row 57: K2tog to end of row [15 sts].
row 58: purl.
row 59: K1, then K2tog to end of row [8 sts].
row 60: purl.
row 61: K2tog to end of row [4 sts].
row 62: purl and cast off.

Making up

1. Fold the torso in half, right sides together. Using backstitch, sew from the top of the head down to 1cm (½in) from the top of the neck.
2. Sew up the centre back seam from the bottom upwards until you are 1cm (½in) from the start of the neck.
3. Turn the work right-side out and stuff the top of the head.

Inserting the backbone

1. Take either a piece of dowelling, a roll of cardboard, an unsharpened pencil or a chopstick that is about 1–2cm (½–¾in) shorter than the combined body and head length of the doll.
2. Wrap sticky tape around it, with the sticky side out, so that it is completely covered.
3. Wrap a fine layer of stuffing along the length of the backbone so that all of the sticky surface is covered.
4. Insert the backbone up through the body and into the head of the doll. Once the backbone is in place, add stuffing through the neck opening and into the head. Shape the head with your fingers until it is a nice, even shape. When you are happy with it, mattress stitch the neck closed.
5. Now continue to stuff the body. Shape the shoulders evenly. When you are finished, whip stitch the base of the body closed.

Ears

Make two.

Cast on 3 sts, leaving a long tail at each end.

row 1: knit, inc each st [6 sts].

row 2: purl.

row 3: knit, inc 1 st at each end [8 sts].

row 4: purl.

row 5: knit, inc 1 st at each end [10 sts].

row 6: purl and cast off.

Making up the ears

1. Place both ears in front of you so that one is the mirror image of the other. The longer side is the outer rim of the ear, so have these facing outwards.

2. For both ears, use the left-over tail thread at the bottom of the ear to make small running stitches around the lobe and up the outer rim. Pull the thread firmly so that the ear lobe becomes rounded in shape. Secure with a small stitch, neaten the thread and cut off. Leave the other tail thread and use it to secure the ear to the side of the head. This should make a fairy-like ear, slightly pointed at the top and round at the bottom.

3. Pin the ears to the side of the head, slightly nearer to the back of the head than to the front. Make sure the two ears are level, and align the side of the ear that will be attached to the head with the edge of the nose. Mattress stitch each ear to the head using the spare tail threads.

4. Make a stitch securing the middle of each ear to the head, thus pinning the ears back so they do not stick out. Neaten the threads and cut off the excess.

Arms

Make two.

Cast on 3 sts.

row 1: knit, inc each st [6 sts].

row 2: purl.

row 3: knit, inc 1 st at each end [8 sts].

rows 4–6: SS for 3 rows, starting with a purl row.

row 7: cast on 3 sts, knit to end [11 sts].

row 8: cast on 3 sts, purl to end [14 sts].

row 9: cast off 3 sts, knit to end [11 sts].

row 10: cast off 3 sts, purl to end [8 sts].

row 11: K2tog, knit to last 2 sts, K2tog [6 sts].

rows 12–40: SS for 29 rows.

row 41: K2tog to end of row [3 sts].

row 42: purl and cast off.

Making up the arms

1. Fold each arm in half lengthwise, wrong sides together, and mattress stitch from the tip of the fingers to 1cm (½in) below the top of the arm. Do not stuff the arms.

2. Pin each arm in place on the body so that the top of each arm is flush with the shoulder. Make sure the arms are evenly placed, then use mattress stitch to sew them in position around the armhole. Neaten the threads and trim them off.

Legs

Each doll has a different pattern for the legs, but they are all made up in the same way. For each leg, fold in half lengthwise, wrong sides together, and mattress stitch up the entire length of the leg. If the legs are to be stuffed, leave a gap at the top for stuffing. Once stuffed, place the legs evenly under the base of the body, making sure the leg seam is at the back. Whip stitch the legs on to the body and neaten and trim the threads.

Rainbow Dream Fairy

There's a magical time after rainfall, when sunbeams and raindrops meet and a rainbow arch of pure colour spreads through the sky. Some believe a pot of gold lies at the end of the rainbow, but no-one has ever been there to find out.

Rainbow Dream Fairy is a happy fairy. She lifts the spirits and promises good times ahead, just like her namesake, and wears a costume in muted tones of all the colours of the rainbow. Knit her for a special friend or relative and you are guaranteed to brighten their day.

You will need

All of the items you need to make the fairies in this book are listed on page 8. The specific yarns, needles, threads and embellishments you need to make Rainbow Dream Fairy are listed below, though you can, of course, use suitable alternatives instead, depending on the style of doll you wish to create and what materials are available to you. Go wherever your imagination takes you!

Yarns:

★ Flesh-coloured and pastel-coloured variegated double-knitting yarn (8-ply/light worsted) for body
★ Variegated eyelash yarn in pastel shades for hair
★ Pink double-knitting yarn (8-ply/light worsted) and fluffy multi-coloured yarn for skirt
★ Variegated double-knitting yarn (8-ply/light worsted) in purple and mauve for wings
★ Small pieces of black eyelash yarn for eyelashes

Needles:

★ 3mm (US 3), 7mm (US 11) and 4mm (US 6) knitting needles

Threads:

★ Light brown embroidery thread for eyebrows

For finishing the fairy:

★ Pink ribbon; about 20 pink glass beads; silver-plated headpin; nylon thread; press-stud for fastening skirt

Torso and head

Using the variegated yarn and 3mm (US 3) needles, cast on 24 sts.

rows 1–10: SS, ending with a purl row.

Waist

row 11: K2tog, K5, K2tog, K6, K2tog, K5, K2tog [20 sts].
rows 12–14: SS for 3 rows, starting with a purl row.
row 15: inc 1 st, K5, inc 1 st, K6, inc 1 st, K5, inc 1 st [24 sts].
rows 16–22: SS for 7 rows.

Shoulders

row 23: K6, inc 2 sts, K8, inc 2 sts, K6 [28 sts].
row 24: purl.
row 25: K6, K2tog twice, K8, K2tog twice, K6 [24 sts].
row 26: P2tog to end of row [12 sts].
row 27: K2tog, knit to last 2 sts, K2tog [10 sts].

Neck

rows 28–34: SS for 7 rows, changing to flesh-coloured yarn at row 32.

Head

Continue in the flesh-coloured yarn.
row 35: knit, inc 1 st at each end [12 sts].
row 36: purl, inc 1 st at each end [14 sts].
row 37: K6, inc 2 sts, K6 [16 sts].
row 38: purl.
row 39: inc 3 sts, K3, inc 4 sts, K3, inc 3 sts [26 sts].
row 40: purl.
row 41: knit, inc 1 st at each end [28 sts].
row 42: purl.
row 43: knit, inc 1 st at each end [30 sts].
rows 44–56: SS for 13 rows.
row 57: K2tog to end of row [15 sts].
row 58: purl.
row 59: K1, then K2tog to end of row [8 sts].
row 60: purl.
row 61: K2tog to end of row [4 sts].
row 62: purl and cast off.

Making up

1. Fold the torso in half, right sides together. Using backstitch, sew from the top of the head down to 1cm (½in) from the top of the neck.
2. Sew up the centre back seam from the bottom until you are 1cm (½in) from the start of the neck.
3. Turn right-side out and stuff the top of the head.

Inserting the backbone

1. Take either a piece of dowelling, a roll of cardboard, an unsharpened pencil or a chopstick that is about 1–2cm (½–¾in) shorter than the combined body and head length of the doll.
2. Wrap sticky tape around it, with the sticky side out, so that it is completely covered.
3. Wrap a fine layer of stuffing along the length of the backbone so that all of the sticky surface is covered.

4. Insert the backbone up through the body and into the head of the doll. Once the backbone is in place, add stuffing through the neck opening and into the head. Shape the head with your fingers until it is a nice, even shape. When you are happy with it, mattress stitch the neck closed.

5. Now continue to stuff the body. Shape the shoulders evenly. When you are finished, whip stitch the base of the body closed.

Ears

Make two.

Using flesh-coloured yarn and 3mm (US 3) needles, cast on 3 sts, leaving a long tail at each end.

row 1: knit, inc each st [6 sts].
row 2: purl.
row 3: knit, inc 1 st at each end [8 sts].
row 4: purl.
row 5: knit, inc 1 st at each end [10 sts].
row 6: purl and cast off.

Making up the ears

You may find it easier to position the ears once you have created the face.

1. Place both ears in front of you so that one is the mirror image of the other. The longer side is the outer rim of the ear, so have these facing outwards.

2. For both ears, use the left-over tail thread at the bottom of the ear to make small running stitches around the lobe and up the outer rim. Pull the thread firmly so that the ear lobe becomes rounded in shape. Secure with a small stitch, neaten the thread and cut off. Leave the other tail thread and use it to secure the ear to the side of the head. This should make a fairy-like ear, slightly pointed at the top and round at the bottom.

3. Pin the ears to the side of the head, slightly nearer to the back of the head than to the front. Make sure the two ears are level, and align the side of the ear that will be attached to the head with the edge of the nose. Mattress stitch each ear to the head using the spare tail threads.

4. Make a stitch securing the middle of each ear to the head, thus pinning the ears back so they do not stick out. Neaten the threads and cut off the excess.

Arms

Make two.

With flesh-coloured yarn and 3mm (US 3) needles, cast on 3 sts.

row 1: knit, inc each st [6 sts].
row 2: purl.
row 3: knit, inc 1 st at each end [8 sts].
rows 4–6: SS for 3 rows.
row 7: cast on 3 sts, knit to end [11 sts].
row 8: cast on 3 sts, purl to end [14 sts].
row 9: cast off 3 sts, knit to end [11 sts].
row 10: cast off 3 sts, purl to end [8 sts].
row 11: K2tog, knit to last 2 sts, K2tog [6 sts].
rows 12–40: SS for 29 rows, changing to variegated yarn at row 13.
row 41: K2tog to end of row [3 sts].
row 42: purl and cast off.

Making up the arms

1. Fold each arm in half lengthwise, wrong sides together, and mattress stitch from the tip of the fingers to 1cm (½in) below the top of the arm. Do not stuff the arms.

2. Pin each arm in place on the body so that the top of each arm is flush with the shoulder. Make sure the arms are evenly placed, then use mattress stitch to sew them in position around the armhole. Neaten the threads and trim them off.

Legs

Make two.

Using the variegated yarn, cast on 3 sts.

row 1: knit, inc each st [6 sts].

row 2: purl.

row 3: knit, inc 1 st at each end [8 sts].

row 4: purl.

row 5: knit, inc 1 st at each end [10 sts].

row 6: purl.

row 7: knit, inc 1 st at each end [12 sts].

rows 8–12: SS for 5 rows.

row 13: K2tog twice, K4, K2tog twice [8 sts].

row 14: purl.

row 15: K2tog, knit to last 2 sts, K2tog [6 sts].

rows 16–62: SS for 47 rows.

Cast off on last purl row.

Making up the legs

1. Fold the legs, wrong sides together, and mattress stitch from the toe to the top of the leg. Do not stuff the female fairy legs.
2. Place the legs evenly under the base of the body, making sure the leg seam is at the back. Whip stitch the legs on to the body and neaten and trim the threads.

Finishing the body

Needlesculpt the body and head following the instructions on page 9.

Face

See pages 9–10 for needlesculpting the face and making the eyes, nose and lips.

For this fairy, I have embroidered her nose from the tip up to the eyes, and coloured her eyes using blue for the irises and brown on the lids. This gives her an innocent, dreamlike quality. Her gently arched eyebrows are embroidered on using light brown embroidery thread, and her rosebud lips are cut from dark red felt. Dab a little pink colour on to the cheeks, and some lilac colour on to the upper part of the eye socket (see page 11).

Eyelashes

Cut a short length of eyelash yarn, about 2cm (¾in) long. Cut it in half and trim each half at an angle so that the eyelashes are shorter at one end than the other. Measure each length of eyelashes against the eyelid and trim to size. Glue each one in place, ensuring the eyelashes are longer on the outside than at the inner eye.

Hair

See the general instructions on page 11. Here I have used a variegated eyelash yarn in colours that match those of the fairy's clothes, though any similar fancy yarn will do.

1. Wind the yarn around a medium-sized book or DVD cover until the desired hair thickness is reached. Cut along one edge.
2. Spread the strands across the back of the fairy's head, spacing them evenly so there are no 'bald' patches. Stitch down the centre back of the head to secure all the strands.
3. Stitch the hair in place around the scalp to secure it firmly. Trim to the required length.

Skirt

Using pink yarn and 7mm (US 11) needles, cast on 68 sts.

rows 1–6: GS.
rows 7–9: change to fluffy yarn and GS for 3 rows.
row 10: change to 4mm (US 6) needles and purl.
row 11: change back to pink yarn and knit.
rows 12–16: SS for 5 rows.
rows 17–18: change to fluffy yarn and GS for 2 rows.
rows 19–32: change back to pink yarn and SS for 14 rows.
row 33: K2tog to end of row [34 sts].
row 34: purl.
row 35: *K1, K2tog*, repeat from * to * to last st, K1 [23 sts].
row 36: purl.
row 37: knit.
row 38: purl and cast off.

Making up the skirt

Fold the skirt in half, right sides facing, and backstitch the seam leaving a 1cm (½in) opening at the waist. Neaten the threads and turn right-side out. Sew a press-stud on to either side of the opening or, if the fairy is not to be undressed, sew the skirt directly on to the body.

Wings

Make two.

Using the purple and mauve variegated yarn and 4mm (US 6) needles, cast on 10 sts.

row 1: knit, inc 1 st at each end [12 sts].

row 2: purl.

rows 3–26: repeat rows 1 and 2 until 36 sts on needle, ending with a purl row.

rows 27–40: SS for 14 rows.

row 41: K2tog, knit to last 2 sts, K2tog [34 sts].

row 42: purl.

rows 43–72: repeat rows 41 and 42 until 4 sts on needle, ending with a purl row.

row 73: K2tog twice and cast off.

Making up the wings

1. Place the two wings together with right sides facing. Stitch them together in the middle, making a seam about 1–2cm (½–¾in) long.

2. Run a line of running stitches across the centre of the outspread wings and pull the thread firmly to gather. This will turn the two wing pieces into four wings – two upper and two lower. Wire the wings, if desired (see page 9).

3. Attach the wings to the fairy with a press-stud, one half sewn on to the right side of the wings in the middle and the other half sewn on to the centre of the fairy's back. Alternatively, sew the wings directly on to her body.

To finish the fairy

Tie a pink ribbon around the fairy's hair, with the bow underneath at the back, and sew on approximately ten glass beads across the front.

Make a choker necklace by first threading three glass beads on to a silver-plated headpin and bending over the top to form a small loop. Thread three beads on to a short length of nylon thread, followed by the headpin, then three further beads. Thread one end of the necklace into a needle and use it to stitch the necklace on to one side of the fairy's neck. Repeat for the other side of the necklace.

Cobweb the Dark Fairy

Even fairyland has a dark side, and this spellbinding creature will cause mayhem wherever she alights. Hiding in nooks and crannies, don't be surprised to find her inhabiting the corner of the garden shed, along with the spiders and other creepy-crawlies she favours.

Her costume of black and purple suggests that even a bad fairy can look glamorous, and the pretty butterfly adornments on her skirt and top show she has a tender side (though she doesn't like to admit it).

You will need

All of the items you need to make the fairies in this book are listed on page 8. The specific yarns, needles, threads and embellishments you need to make Cobweb are listed below, though you can, of course, use suitable alternatives instead, depending on the style of doll you wish to create and what materials are available to you.

Yarns:

* Purple, black and flesh-coloured double-knitting yarn (8-ply/light worsted) for body
* Dark brown eyelash yarn for hair
* Black, light DK (5-ply/sport) yarn for skirt
* Sparkly black, light DK (5-ply/sport) yarn for wings

Needles:

* 3mm (US 3), 7mm (US 11) and 4mm (US 6) knitting needles

Threads:

* Dark brown embroidery thread for eyebrows and mole

For finishing the fairy:

* Fine black ribbon for skirt ties (optional); black, fine feather boa and small butterfly charms for embellishing the skirt; black and silver fine feather boa and purple silk flowers for decorating hair; two large butterfly embellishments; purple ribbon for choker necklace; black sewing thread; two black beads for earrings; two decorative black bows for feet.

Torso and head

Using the purple yarn and 3mm (US 3) needles, cast on 24 sts.

rows 1–10: SS, ending with a purl row.

Waist

row 11: K2tog, K5, K2tog, K6, K2tog, K5, K2tog [20 sts].
rows 12–14: SS for 3 rows.
row 15: inc 1 st, K5, inc 1 st, K6, inc 1 st, K5, inc 1 st [24 sts].
rows 16–20: SS for 5 rows.
row 21: K11, then K2 in flesh-coloured yarn, K11 in purple.
row 22: P10 purple, P4 flesh-coloured, P10 purple.

Shoulders

row 23: K6 purple, inc 2 sts, K1, change to flesh-coloured yarn and K6, change back to purple and K1, inc 2 sts, K6 [28 sts].
row 24: P10 purple, P8 flesh-coloured, P10 purple.
row 25: K6 purple, K2tog, change to flesh-coloured yarn and K2tog, K8, K2tog, change back to purple and K2tog, K6 [24 sts].
row 26: P2tog using flesh colour to end of row [12 sts].
row 27: K2tog, knit to last 2 sts, K2tog [10 sts].

Neck

rows 28–34: SS for 7 rows, changing to flesh-coloured yarn at row 32.

Head

Continue in the flesh-coloured yarn.
row 35: knit, inc 1 st at each end [12 sts].
row 36: purl, inc 1 st at each end [14 sts].
row 37: K6, inc 2 sts, K6 [16 sts].
row 38: purl.
row 39: inc 3 sts, K3, inc 4 sts, K3, inc 3 sts [26 sts].
row 40: purl.
row 41: knit, inc 1 st at each end [28 sts].
row 42: purl.
row 43: knit, inc 1 st at each end [30 sts].
rows 44–56: SS for 13 rows.
row 57: K2tog to end of row [15 sts].
row 58: purl.
row 59: K1, then K2tog to end of row [8 sts].
row 60: purl.
row 61: K2tog to end of row [4 sts].
row 62: purl and cast off.

Making up

1. Fold the torso in half, right sides together. Using backstitch, sew from the top of the head down to 1cm (½in) from the top of the neck.
2. Sew up the centre back seam from the bottom until you are 1cm (½in) from the start of the neck.
3. Turn the work right-side out and stuff the top of the head.

Inserting the backbone

1. Take either a piece of dowelling, a roll of cardboard, an unsharpened pencil or a chopstick that is about 1–2cm (½–¾in) shorter than the combined body and head length of the doll.
2. Wrap sticky tape around it, with the sticky side out, so that it is completely covered.
3. Wrap a fine layer of stuffing along the length of the backbone so that all of the sticky surface is covered.
4. Insert the backbone up through the body and into the head of the doll. Once the backbone is in place, add stuffing through the neck opening and into the head. Shape the head with your fingers until it is a nice, even shape. When you are happy with it, mattress stitch the neck closed.
5. Now continue to stuff the body. Shape the shoulders evenly. When you are finished, whip stitch the base of the body closed.

Ears

Make two.
With flesh-coloured and 3mm (US 3) needles, cast on 3 sts, leaving a long tail at each end.
row 1: knit, inc each st [6 sts].
row 2: purl.
row 3: knit, inc 1 st at each end [8 sts].
row 4: purl.
row 5: knit, inc 1 st at each end [10 sts].
row 6: purl and cast off.

Making up the ears

You may find it easier to position the ears once you have created the face.

1. Place both ears in front of you so that one is the mirror image of the other. The longer side is the outer rim of the ear, so have these facing outwards.
2. For both ears, use the left-over tail thread at the bottom of the ear to make small running stitches around the lobe and up the outer rim. Pull the thread firmly so that the ear lobe becomes rounded in shape. Secure with a small stitch, neaten the thread and cut off. Leave the other tail thread and use it to secure the ear to the side of the head. This should make a fairy-like ear, slightly pointed at the top and round at the bottom.
3. Pin the ears to the side of the head, slightly nearer to the back of the head than to the front. Make sure the two ears are level, and align the side of the ear that will be attached to the head with the edge of the

nose. Mattress stitch each ear to the head using the spare tail threads.
4. Make a stitch securing the middle of each ear to the head, thus pinning the ears back so they do not stick out. Neaten the threads and cut off the excess.

Arms

Make two.
Using flesh-coloured yarn and 3mm (US 3) needles, cast on 3 sts using flesh-coloured yarn.
row 1: knit, inc each st [6 sts].
row 2: purl.
row 3: knit, inc 1 st at each end [8 sts].
rows 4–6: SS for 3 rows.
row 7: cast on 3 sts, knit to end [11 sts].
row 8: cast on 3 sts, purl to end [14 sts].
row 9: cast off 3 sts, knit to end [11 sts].
row 10: cast off 3 sts, purl to end [8 sts].
row 11: K2tog, knit to last 2 sts, K2tog [6 sts].
rows 12–40: SS for 29 rows.
row 41: K2tog to end of row [3 sts].
row 42: purl and cast off.

Making up the arms

1. Fold each arm in half lengthwise, wrong sides together, and mattress stitch from the tip of the fingers to 1cm (½in) below the top of the arm. Do not stuff the arms.
2. Pin each arm in place on the body so that the top of each arm is flush with the shoulder. Make sure the arms are evenly placed, then use mattress stitch to sew them in position around the armhole. Neaten the threads and trim them off.

Legs

Make two.
Using black yarn and 3mm (US 3) needles, cast on 3 sts.
row 1: knit, inc each st [6 sts].
row 2: purl.
row 3: knit, inc 1 st at each end [8 sts].
row 4: purl.
row 5: knit, inc 1 st at each end [10 sts].
row 6: purl.
row 7: knit, inc 1 st at each end [12 sts].
rows 8–12: SS for 5 rows.
row 13: K2tog twice, K4, K2tog twice [8 sts].
row 14: purl.
row 15: K2tog, knit to last 2 sts, K2tog [6 sts].
rows 16–31: SS for 16 rows.
rows 32–62: introduce the purple yarn and purl 1 row, then alternate the colours, using purple on every purl row and black on every knit row.
Cast off on last purl row.

Making up the legs

1. Fold the legs, wrong sides together, and mattress stitch from the toe to the top of the leg. Do not stuff the female fairy legs.
2. Place the legs evenly under the base of the body, making sure the leg seam is at the back. Whip stitch the legs on to the body and neaten and trim the threads.

Finishing the body

Needlesculpt the body and head following the instructions on page 9.

Face

See pages 9–10 for needlesculpting the face and making the eyes, nose and lips.

Cobweb's nose is embroidered from the tip up to the eyes, and her heavy-lidded eyes are coloured deep blue for the irises and brown on the lids. Her arched eyebrows are embroidered on using dark brown embroidery thread, and her red rosebud lips are cut from dark red felt. Leave her cheeks pale, and dab some dark grey colour on to the upper part of the eye socket (see page 11). Complete Cobweb's face by stitching a small mole on to her left cheek.

Hair

1. Wind a length of dark brown eyelash yarn around five fingers until it forms a soft ball. Cut off the yarn and stitch the ball to the fairy's head to form a soft, loose bun.
2. For her ponytail, wind yarn around a large book to obtain the length of hair you want. Cut through the loops along one edge. Fold the strands in half and stitch them firmly into the middle of the bun.

Skirt

Using black, light DK (5-ply/sport) yarn and 4mm (US 6) needles, cast on 110 sts.

rows 1–5: GS.

rows 6–16: SS for 11 rows, starting with a purl row.

row 17: K2tog to end of row [55 sts].

row 18: purl.

row 19: *K1, K2tog*, repeat from * to * to last st, K1 [37 sts].

row 20: purl.

row 21: *K1, K2tog*, repeat from * to * to last st, K1 [25 sts].

row 22: purl and cast off.

Making up the skirt

1. Neaten all the loose threads. Crochet 2 chains, each 10cm (4in) long, or knit 2 chains using knit 1 st, turn, knit 1 st. Alternatively, use lengths of fine ribbon. Attach a chain to either side of the waist. Wrap the skirt around the fairy and tie it in place.

2. To finish off, sew a length of fine feather boa around the skirt's lower edge using black cotton thread and attach the small butterfly charms.

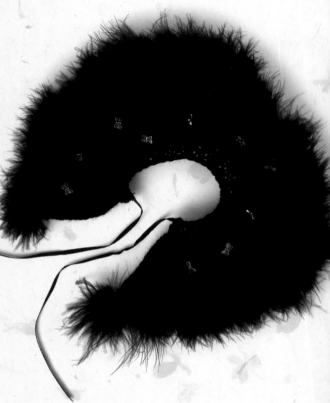

Wings

Right upper wing

Using sparkly black, light DK (5-ply/sport) yarn and 3mm (US 3) needles, cast on 8 sts.

row 1: knit, inc 1 st at end of row [9 sts].

row 2: purl.

rows 3–20: repeat rows 1 and 2 nine times until 18 sts on needle, ending with a purl row.

row 21: knit.

row 22: (purl row) cast on 4 sts, purl to end [22 sts].

row 23: K2tog, knit to last st, inc 1 st [22 sts].

row 24: purl.

rows 25–28: repeat rows 23 and 24 twice.

row 29: knit, inc 1 st at each end of row [24 sts].

row 30: purl.

rows 31–42: repeat rows 29 and 30 until 36 sts on needle, ending with a purl row.

row 43: K2tog, knit to last 2 sts, K2tog [34 sts].

row 44: purl.

rows 45–76: repeat rows 43 and 44 until 2 sts rem. Cast off on row 76.

Left upper wing

Using sparkly black, light DK (5-ply/sport) and 3mm (US 3) needles, cast on 8 sts.

row 1: knit, inc 1 st, knit to end of row [9 sts].

row 2: purl.

rows 3–20: repeat rows 1 and 2 until 18 sts on needle, ending with a purl row.

row 21: (knit row) cast on 4 sts, knit to end [22 sts].

row 22: purl.

row 23: inc 1 st, knit to last 2 sts, K2tog [22 sts].

row 24: purl.

rows 25–28: repeat rows 23 and 24 twice.

row 29: knit, inc 1 st at each end of row [24 sts].

row 30: purl.

rows 31–42: repeat rows 29 and 30 until 36 sts on needle, ending with a purl row.

row 43: K2tog, knit to last 2 sts, K2tog [34 sts].

row 44: purl.

rows 45–76: repeat rows 43 and 44 until 2 sts rem. Cast off on row 76.

Lower right wing

Using sparkly black, light DK (5-ply/sport) yarn and 3mm (US 3) needles, cast on 8 sts.

row 1: knit, inc 1 st, knit to end of row [9 sts].

row 2: purl.

rows 3–28: repeat rows 1 and 2 until 22 sts on needle, ending with a purl row.

row 29: K2tog, knit to last 2 sts, K2tog [20 sts].

row 30: purl.

rows 31–46: repeat rows 29 and 30 until 4 sts rem, ending with a purl row.

rows 47–56: SS for 10 rows.

row 57: K2tog twice [2 sts].

rows 58–66: SS for 9 rows.

row 67: K2tog and cast off.

Lower left wing

Using sparkly black, light DK (5-ply/sport) and 3mm (US 3) needles, cast on 8 sts.

row 1: knit, inc 1 st at end of row [9 sts].

row 2: purl.

rows 3–24: repeat rows 1 and 2 until 22 sts on needle, ending with a purl row.

row 25: K2tog, knit to last 2 sts, K2tog [20 sts].

row 26: purl.

rows 27–42: repeat rows 25 and 26 until 4 sts rem, ending with a purl row.

rows 43–52: SS for 10 rows.

row 53: K2tog twice [2 sts].

rows 54–62: SS for 9 rows.

row 63: K2tog and cast off.

Making up the wings

1. Neaten all the loose threads and place the two upper wings together, right sides facing. Stitch them together in the middle, making a seam about 1–2cm (½–¾in) long. Repeat for the lower wings.

2. Place the lower wings with right sides up. Place the upper wings on top of them, right sides together and with the top of the upper wings aligned with the bottom of the lower wings. Stitch the two sets of wings together for 2–4cm (¾–1½in).

3. For unwired wings, sew one half of a press-stud on to the front of the wings in the middle, and the other half on to the centre of the fairy's back. Alternatively, attach the wings directly on to the fairy.

   For wired wings, do not sew on a press-stud. Instead, lay the wings out flat and, using fine florists' wire, bend the wire into the shape of the wings. Start where the two sets of wings are joined and bend the wire first round the upper wings and then the lower wings (leave the trailing ends of the lower wings unwired). Leave a 10cm (4in) tail of wire at each end. Stitch the wire in place using a mattress stitch (see page 9). Bring the excess wire to the front and form it into two loops that are just large enough to fit comfortably round the fairy's arms. Bend the ends of the wire over.

To finish the fairy

Tie a length of fine, sparkly feather boa around the fairy's head, then stitch together a line of purple silk flowers and wrap them around the top of her ponytail.

Attach two large butterfly embellishments to the top of her bodice, and tie a length of purple ribbon around her neck to form a choker necklace. For each earring, pass a length of black sewing thread through the fairy's earlobe, thread on a black bead, and pass the thread back through the same hole, leaving the bead dangling. Secure the thread.

Finally, stitch a decorative black bow to the front of each foot.

Blue Moon Fairy

On quiet moonlit nights, Blue Moon Fairy can often be seen flitting silently between the moonbeams, alighting here and there while people, all around her, are fast asleep. She is a shy creature, and loves the peace and solitude that night time brings after the hustle and bustle of the day.

Blue Moon is a gentle, mystical fairy, reflected in her long, soft blue hair, delicate wings and large, hypnotic blue eyes. Peep out through the curtains next time you hear a rustling in the garden late at night, and if you are lucky you might just catch a glimpse of her.

You will need

All of the items you need to make the fairies in this book
are listed on page 8. The specific yarns, needles, threads
and embellishments you need to make Blue Moon Fairy
are listed below, though you can, of course, use suitable
alternatives instead, depending on the style of doll you wish
to create and what materials are available to you.

Yarns:

★ Flesh-coloured and pastel-coloured variegated
   double-knitting yarn (8-ply/light worsted)
   for body
★ Blue, variegated eyelash yarn for hair
★ Sparkly blue double-knitting yarn (8-ply/light
   worsted) for lower legs and skirt
★ Turquoise double-knitting yarn (8-ply/light
   worsted) for wings

Needles:

★ 3mm (US 3), 7mm (US 11) and 4mm (US 6)
   knitting needles

Threads:

★ Light brown embroidery thread for eyebrows

For finishing the fairy:

★ Pale green tassel fringe for tying up hair; about
   36 glass beads in light and dark pink

Torso and head

Using the variegated yarn and 3mm (US 3) needles, cast on 24 sts.

rows 1–10: SS, ending with a purl row.

Waist

row 11: K2tog, K5, K2tog, K6, K2tog, K5, K2tog [20 sts].

rows 12–14: SS for 3 rows, starting with a purl row.

row 15: inc 1 st, K5, inc 1 st, K6, inc 1 st, K5, inc 1 st [24 sts].

rows 16–22: SS for 7 rows, starting with a purl row.

Shoulders

row 23: K6, inc 2 sts, K8, inc 2 sts, K6 [28 sts].

row 24: purl.

row 25: K6, K2tog twice, K8, K2tog twice, K6 [24 sts].

row 26: P2tog to end of row [12 sts].

row 27: K2tog, knit to last 2 sts, K2tog [10 sts].

Neck

rows 28–34: SS for 7 rows.

Head

Change to flesh-coloured yarn.

row 35: knit, inc 1 st at each end [12 sts].

row 36: purl, inc 1 st at each end [14 sts].

row 37: K6, inc 2 sts, K6 [16 sts].

row 38: purl.

row 39: inc 3 sts, K3, inc 4 sts, K3, inc 3 sts [26 sts].

row 40: purl.

row 41: knit, inc 1 st at each end [28 sts].

row 42: purl.

row 43: knit, inc 1 st at each end [30 sts].

rows 44–56: SS for 13 rows.

row 57: K2tog to end of row [15 sts].

row 58: purl.

row 59: K1, then K2tog to end of row [8 sts].

row 60: purl.

row 61: K2tog to end of row [4 sts].

row 62: purl and cast off.

Making up

1. Fold the torso in half, right sides together. Using backstitch, sew from the top of the head down to 1cm (½in) from the top of the neck.
2. Sew up the centre back seam from the bottom until you are 1cm (½in) from the start of the neck.
3. Turn the work right-side out and stuff the top of the head.

Inserting the backbone

1. Take either a piece of dowelling, a roll of cardboard, an unsharpened pencil or a chopstick that is about 1–2cm (½–¾in) shorter than the combined body and head length of the doll.
2. Wrap sticky tape around it, with the sticky side out, so that it is completely covered.
3. Wrap a fine layer of stuffing along the length of the backbone so that all of the sticky surface is covered.
4. Insert the backbone up through the body and into the head of the doll. Once the backbone is in place, add stuffing through the neck opening and into the head. Shape the head with your fingers until it is a nice, even shape. When you are happy with it, mattress stitch the neck closed.
5. Now continue to stuff the body. Shape the shoulders evenly. When you are finished, whip stitch the base of the body closed.

Ears

Make two.
Using flesh-coloured yarn and 3mm (US 3) needles, cast on 3 sts, leaving a long tail at each end.
row 1: knit, inc each st [6 sts].
row 2: purl.
row 3: knit, inc 1 st at each end [8 sts].
row 4: purl.
row 5: knit, inc 1 st at each end [10 sts].
row 6: purl and cast off.

Making up the ears

You may find it easier to position the ears once you have created the face.

1. Place both ears in front of you so that one is the mirror image of the other. The longer side is the outer rim of the ear, so have these facing outwards.
2. For both ears, use the left-over tail thread at the bottom of the ear to make small running stitches around the lobe and up the outer rim. Pull the thread firmly so that the ear lobe becomes rounded in shape. Secure with a small stitch, neaten the thread and cut off. Leave the other tail thread and use it to secure the ear to the side of the head. This should make a fairy-like ear, slightly pointed at the top and round at the bottom.

3. Pin the ears to the side of the head, slightly nearer to the back of the head than to the front. Make sure the two ears are level, and align the side of the ear that will be attached to the head with the edge of the nose. Mattress stitch each ear to the head using the spare tail threads.
4. Make a stitch securing the middle of each ear to the head, thus pinning the ears back so they do not stick out. Neaten the threads and cut off the excess.

Arms

Make two.

Using flesh-coloured yarn and 3mm (US 3) needles, cast on 3 sts using flesh-coloured yarn.

row 1: knit, inc each st [6 sts].

row 2: purl.

row 3: knit, inc 1 st at each end [8 sts].

rows 4–6: SS for 3 rows, starting with a purl row.

row 7: cast on 3 sts, knit to end [11 sts].

row 8: cast on 3 sts, purl to end [14 sts].

row 9: cast off 3 sts, knit to end [11 sts].

row 10: cast off 3 sts, purl to end [8 sts].

row 11: K2tog, knit to last 2 sts, K2tog [6 sts].

rows 12–40: SS for 29 rows.

row 41: K2tog to end of row [3 sts].

row 42: purl and cast off.

Making up the arms

1. Fold each arm in half lengthwise, wrong sides together, and mattress stitch from the tip of the fingers to 1cm (½in) below the top of the arm. Do not stuff the arms.

2. Pin each arm in place on the body so that the top of each arm is flush with the shoulder. Make sure the arms are evenly placed, then use mattress stitch to sew them in position around the armhole. Neaten the threads and trim them off.

Legs

Make two.

Using sparkly blue yarn and 3mm (US 3) needles, cast on 3 sts.

row 1: knit, inc each st [6 sts].

row 2: purl.

row 3: knit, inc 1 st at each end [8 sts].

row 4: purl.

row 5: knit, inc 1 st at each end [10 sts].

row 6: purl.

row 7: knit, inc 1 st at each end [12 sts].

rows 8–12: SS for 5 rows.

row 13: K2tog twice, K4, K2tog twice [8 sts].

row 14: purl.

row 15: K2tog, knit to last 2 sts, K2tog [6 sts].

rows 16–31: SS for 16 rows.

rows 32–62: introduce the variegated yarn and SS for 31 rows.

Cast off on last purl row.

Making up the legs

1. Fold the legs, wrong sides together, and mattress stitch from the toe to the top of the leg. Do not stuff the female fairy legs.
2. Place the legs evenly under the base of the body, making sure the leg seam is at the back. Whip stitch the legs on to the body and neaten and trim the threads.

Finishing the body

Needlesculpt the body and head following the instructions on page 9.

Face

See pages 9–10 for needlesculpting the face and making the eyes, nose and lips.

I have embroidered Blue Moon Fairy's nose from the tip up to the eyes, and coloured her eyes using blue for the irises and brown on the lids. The eyes are attached so that the outer edges slant upwards slightly, giving her a mystical appearance. Her gently arched eyebrows are embroidered on using light brown embroidery thread, and her rosebud lips are cut from dark red felt. Dab a little pink colour on to the cheeks, and some pale blue colour on to the upper part of the eye socket (see page 11). This accentuates her dreamlike quality.

Hair

See the general instructions on page 11. Here I have used a blue, variegated eyelash yarn, though any similar fancy yarn will do.

1. Wind the yarn around a large book to obtain the length of hair you want, and cut along one edge.
2. Take each strand in turn, fold it in half and hook it through a single knitted stitch on the fairy's scalp with a crochet hook.
3. Once the head is covered in a good, thick layer of hair, tie the hair up to one side in a high pony tail with a piece of tassel fringe.
4. Trim the hair to the correct length if desired.

Skirt

With sparkly blue yarn and 4mm (US 6) needles, cast on 20 sts.
rows 1–2: SS for 2 rows.
row 3: knit, inc 1 st at each end of row [22 sts].
row 4: purl.
row 5: knit, inc 1 st at each end of row [24 sts].
rows 6–14: SS for 9 rows.
row 15: K2tog, knit to last 2 sts, K2tog [22 sts].
row 16: purl.
row 17: K2tog, knit to last 2 sts, K2tog [20 sts].
row 18: purl and cast off.

Making up the skirt

Fold the skirt in half, right sides together, and backstitch up the seam. Neaten the threads and turn right-side out. Pull the skirt up over the fairy's hips.

Wings

Using turquoise yarn and 4mm (US 6) needles, cast on 40 sts.
rows 1–3: GS.
rows 4–6: SS for 3 rows, starting with a purl row.
row 7: K2tog to end of row [20 sts].
rows 8–18: SS for 11 rows, startin with a purl row.
row 19: K2tog to end of row [10 sts].
row 20: purl.
row 21: knit, inc 1 in each st [20 sts].
rows 22–32: SS for 11 rows, starting with a purl row.
row 33: knit, inc 1 in each st [40 sts].
rows 34–36: SS for 3 rows, starting with a purl row.
rows 37–39: GS. Cast off on row 39.

Making up the wings

1. Place the knitting with the garter-stitch edges at the sides and make two parallel lines of running stitch from one side to the other. Pull the thread firmly to gather the knitting into the shape of the wings. Secure and neaten the threads.

2. Wire the wings if desired (see page 9).

3. Sew on a press-stud, with one half on the top of the wings in the middle and the other in the centre of the fairy's back. Alternatively, sew the wings directly on to the fairy.

To finish the fairy

Stitch glass beads around the edge of the tassel fringe used to tie up the fairy's hair, alternating light and dark pink beads. Stitch the same types of bead around her neck, in a zig-zag pattern, and sew one bead on each earlobe for matching earrings.

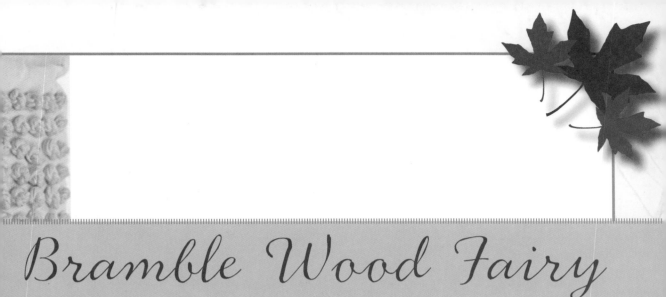

Bramble Wood Fairy

Next time you are out searching the hedgerows for berries and fruit, look out for Bramble Wood Fairy hiding in amongst the leaves. His leaf-like wings mean he is well camouflaged, though you might catch sight of his shock of bright blue hair. This mischievous elfin fairy has a flamboyant nature, and loves to wear his stout brown boots with a blue trim to match his blue hair.

You will need

All of the items you need to make the fairies in this book are listed on page 8. The specific yarns, needles, threads and embellishments you need to make Bramble Wood Fairy are listed below, though you can, of course, use suitable alternatives instead, depending on the style of doll you wish to create and what materials are available to you.

Yarns:

* Sparkly brown, black and flesh-coloured double-knitting yarn (8-ply/light worsted) for body
* Blue eyelash yarn for trim on legs
* Blue fluffy yarn or fine feather boa for hair
* Fine, silky yarn in two shades of brown for coat
* Green and blue variegated double-knitting yarn (8-ply/light worsted) for wings

Needles:

* 3mm (US 3), 7mm (US 11) and 4mm (US 6) knitting needles

Threads:

* Dark brown embroidery thread for eyebrows

For finishing the fairy:

* Press-stud for fastening coat; two large silk leaves for wings; about 18 small gold beads

Torso and head

Using the sparkly brown yarn and 3mm (US 3) needles, cast on 24 sts.

rows 1–10: SS, ending with a purl row.

Waist

row 11: K2tog, K5, K2tog, K6, K2tog, K5, K2tog [20 sts].
rows 12–14: SS for 3 rows.
row 15: inc 1 st, K5, inc 1 st, K6, inc 1 st, K5, inc 1 st [24 sts].
rows 16–22: SS for 7 rows.

Shoulders

row 23: K6, inc 2 sts, K8, inc 2 sts, K6 [28 sts].
row 24: purl.
row 25: K6, K2tog twice, K8, K2tog twice, K6 [24 sts].
row 26: P2tog to end of row [12 sts].
row 27: K2tog, knit to last 2 sts, K2tog [10 sts].

Neck

Change to flesh-coloured yarn.
rows 28–34: SS for 7 rows.

Head

row 35: knit, inc 1 st at each end [12 sts].
row 36: purl, inc 1 st at each end [14 sts].
row 37: K6, inc 2 sts, K6 [16 sts].
row 38: purl.
row 39: inc 3 sts, K3, inc 4 sts, K3, inc 3 sts [26 sts].
row 40: purl.
row 41: knit, inc 1 st at each end [28 sts].

row 42: purl.
row 43: knit, inc 1 st at each end [30 sts].
rows 44–56: SS for 13 rows.
row 57: K2tog to end of row [15 sts].
row 58: purl.
row 59: K1, then K2tog to end of row [8 sts].
row 60: purl.
row 61: K2tog to end of row [4 sts].
row 62: purl and cast off.

Making up

1. Fold the torso in half, right sides together. Using backstitch, sew from the top of the head down to 1cm (½in) from the top of the neck.
2. Sew up the centre back seam from the bottom upwards until you are 1cm (½in) from the start of the neck.
3. Turn right-side out and stuff the top of the head.

Inserting the backbone

1. Take either a piece of dowelling, a roll of cardboard, an unsharpened pencil or a chopstick that is about 1–2cm (½–¾in) shorter than the combined body and head length of the doll.
2. Wrap sticky tape around it, with the sticky side out, so that it is completely covered.
3. Wrap a fine layer of stuffing along the length of the backbone so that all of the sticky surface is covered.
4. Insert the backbone up through the body and into the head of the doll. Once the backbone is in place, add stuffing through the neck opening and into the head. Shape the head with your fingers until it is a nice, even shape. When you are happy with it, mattress stitch the neck closed.
5. Now continue to stuff the body. Shape the shoulders evenly. When you are finished, whip stitch the base of the body closed.

Ears

Make two.
With flesh-coloured yarn and 3mm (US 3) needles, cast on 3 sts, leaving a long tail at each end.
Row 1: knit, inc each st [6 sts].
Row 2: purl.
Row 3: knit, inc 1 st at each end [8 sts].
Row 4: purl.
Row 5: knit, inc 1 st at each end [10 sts].
Row 6: purl and cast off.

Making up the ears

You may find it easier to position the ears once you have created the face.

1. Place both ears in front of you so that one is the mirror image of the other. The longer side is the outer rim of the ear, so have these facing outwards.
2. For both ears, use the left-over tail thread at the bottom of the ear to make small running stitches around the lobe and up the outer rim. Pull the thread firmly so that the ear lobe becomes rounded in shape. Secure with a small stitch, neaten the thread and cut off. Leave the other tail thread and use it to secure the ear to the side of the head. This should make a fairy-like ear, slightly pointed at the top and round at the bottom.
3. Pin the ears to the side of the head, slightly nearer to the back of the head than to the front. Make sure the two ears are level, and align the side of the ear that will be attached to the head with the edge of the nose. Mattress stitch each ear to the head using the spare tail threads.
4. Make a stitch securing the middle of each ear to the head, thus pinning the ears back so they do not stick out. Neaten the threads and cut off the excess.

Arms

Make two.
Using flesh-coloured yarn and 3mm (US 3) needles, cast on 3 sts.
row 1: knit, inc each st [6 sts].
row 2: purl.
row 3: knit, inc 1 st at each end [8 sts].
rows 4–6: SS for 3 rows, starting with a purl row.
row 7: cast on 3 sts, knit to end [11 sts].
row 8: cast on 3 sts, purl to end [14 sts].
row 9: cast off 3 sts, knit to end [11 sts].
row 10: cast off 3 sts, purl to end [8 sts].
row 11: K2tog, knit to last 2 sts, K2tog [6 sts].
rows 12–40: change to sparkly brown yarn and SS for 29 rows.
row 41: K2tog to end of row [3 sts].
row 42: purl and cast off.

Making up the arms

1. Fold each arm in half lengthwise, wrong sides together, and mattress stitch from the tip of the fingers to 1cm (½in) below the top of the arm. Do not stuff the arms.
2. Pin each arm in place on the body so that the top of each arm is flush with the shoulder. Make sure the arms are evenly placed, then use mattress stitch to sew them in position around the armhole. Neaten the threads and trim them off.

Legs

Make two.
Using sparkly brown yarn, cast on 3 sts.
row 1: knit, inc each st across row [6 sts].
row 2: purl.
row 3: knit, inc 1 st at each end [8 sts].
row 4: purl.
rows 5–12: repeat rows 3 and 4 until 16 sts on needle, ending with a purl row.
rows 13–16: SS for 4 rows.
row 17: K2tog twice, K8, K2tog twice [12 sts].
row 18: purl.
row 19: K2tog twice, K4, K2 tog twice [8 sts].

rows 20–24: SS for 5 rows, starting with a purl row.
row 25: inc 1 st, knit to end of row [9 sts].
row 26: inc 1 st, purl to end of row [10 sts].
rows 27–28: repeat rows 25 and 26 [12 sts].
rows 29–36: SS for 8 rows.
rows 37–42: change to blue eyelash yarn and GS for 6 rows.
rows 43–72: change to black yarn and SS for 30 rows. Cast off on last row.

Making up the legs

1. Fold the legs, wrong sides together, and mattress stitch from the toe to the top of the leg. Stuff the legs firmly but don't over stuff.
2. Place the legs evenly under the base of the body, making sure the leg seam is at the back. Whip stitch the legs on to the body and neaten and trim the threads.

Finishing the body

Needlesculpt the body and head following the instructions on page 9.

Face

See pages 9–10 for needlesculpting the face and making the eyes, nose and lips.

Bramble Wood Fairy's nose is embroidered from the tip up to the eyes, and his eyes are coloured using brown for the irises and brown on the lids. His straight eyebrows are embroidered on fairly high on his forehead using dark brown embroidery thread, and his red lips are cut from dark red felt.

Hair

Cut a small length of blue fluffy yarn or trim, such as fine feather boa, and coil it around on the top of the fairy's head. Once it is arranged as you'd like it, pin it in place. Stitch the hair to the scalp with a needle and sewing thread.

Coat

Knitted from the collar down.
Working with two strands of fine, silky yarn in two different shades of brown and 3mm (US 3) needles, cast on 40 sts.
rows 1–6: GS.
row 7: K2tog twice, knit to last 4 sts, K2tog twice [36 sts].
rows 8–15: repeat row 7 until 4 sts rem.
row 16: cast on 4 sts and knit to end [8 sts].
row 17: cast on 4 sts and knit to end [12 sts].
row 18: knit, inc 1 st at each end [14 sts].
row 19: knit.
row 20: knit, inc 1 st at each end [16 sts].
row 21: knit.
row 22: inc 1 st, K7, turn and work on these 9 sts only.
row 23: knit, inc 1 st at each end [11 sts].
row 24: knit.
rows 25–32: repeat rows 23 and 24 until 19 sts on needle.
rows 33–36: GS for 5 rows.
row 37: K2tog, knit to last 2 sts, K2tog [17 sts].
rows 38–44: repeat row 37 until 3 sts rem.
row 45: cast off.
row 46: return to remaining 8 sts and knit to last st, inc into last stitch [9 sts].
Follow pattern from row 23 onwards.

Making up the coat

Lay the coat out flat, wrong side facing upwards, with the collar at the top. Fold one lower corner of the collar down and stitch it to a point mid-way along the body of the coat. Repeat on the other side. This forms the armholes as well as the collar. Place the coat on the fairy and fold one side of the coat over the other. Sew a press-stud on to the front of one side and the inside of the other to hold it in place.

Wings

Using green and blue variegated yarn and 4mm (US 6) needles, cast on 3 sts.

row 1: inc each stitch [6 sts].
row 2: purl.
row 3: knit, inc 1 st at each end of row [8 sts].
row 4: purl.
rows 5–8: repeat rows 3 and 4 until 12 sts on needle, ending with a purl row.
rows 9–26: SS for 18 rows, starting with a knit row.
row 27: K4, K2tog twice, K4 [10 sts].
rows 28–32: SS for 5 rows, starting with a purl row.
row 33: K3, K2tog twice, K3 [8 sts].
rows 34–38: SS for 5 rows, starting with a purl row.
row 39: K2, K2tog twice, K2 [6 sts].
rows 40–42: SS for 3 rows, starting with a purl row.
row 43: K1, K2tog twice, K1 [4 sts].
row 44: purl.
row 45: K2tog twice and cast off.

Making up the wings

1. Wire the wings, if you wish, with either fine floristry wire or chenille sticks (see page 9).
2. Attach two large silk leaves to the knitted wings to form the lower wings.
3. Sew on a press-stud, with one half on the top of the wings in the middle and the other in the centre of the fairy's back. Make sure it isn't covered by the fairy's coat. Alternatively, sew the wings directly on to the fairy.

To finish the fairy

Sew small gold beads to the corner of each knitted wing, approximately nine on each side.

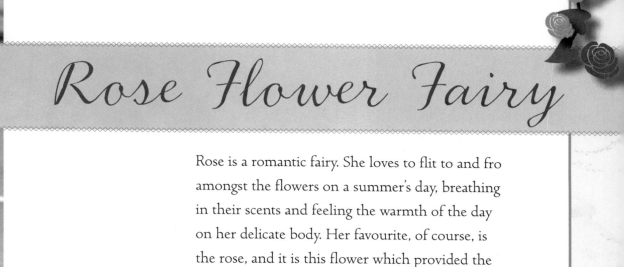

Rose Flower Fairy

Rose is a romantic fairy. She loves to flit to and fro amongst the flowers on a summer's day, breathing in their scents and feeling the warmth of the day on her delicate body. Her favourite, of course, is the rose, and it is this flower which provided the inspiration for her pretty dress. Her dainty wings are multi-coloured, and you might well mistake her for a shimmering butterfly as she flutters amongst the flowerbeds.

You will need

All of the items you need to make the fairies in this book are listed on page 8. The specific yarns, needles, threads and embellishments you need to make Rose Flower Fairy are listed below, though you can, of course, use suitable alternatives instead, depending on the style of doll you wish to create and what materials are available to you.

Yarns:

★ Pink and flesh-coloured double-knitting yarn (8-ply/light worsted) for body
★ Variegated eyelash yarn in browns, pinks and purples for hair
★ Pink light DK (5-ply/sport) yarn for clothes
★ Variegated double-knitting yarn (8-ply/light worsted) in pinks, purples and greens for wings

Needles:

★ 3mm (US 3), 7mm (US 11) and 4mm (US 6) knitting needles

Threads:

★ Dark brown embroidery thread for eyebrows and eyelashes

For finishing the fairy:

★ About 10 large shiny beads in shades of pink to finish skirt; variety of small glass beads in shades of pink; fine wire and silver-plated headpin for necklace; nylon thread and various pink beads for hair decoration; four larger glass beads for necklace and earrings

Torso and head

Using pink yarn and 3mm (US 3) needles, cast on 24 sts.
rows 1–10: SS, ending with a purl row.

Waist

row 11: K2tog, K5, K2tog, K6, K2tog, K5, K2tog [20 sts].
rows 12–14: SS for 3 rows.
row 15: inc 1 st, K5, inc 1 st, K6, inc 1 st, K5, inc 1 st [24 sts].
rows 16–22: SS for 7 rows.

Shoulders

row 23: K6, inc 2 sts, K8, inc 2 sts, K6 [28 sts].
row 24: purl.
row 25: K6, K2tog twice, K8, K2tog twice, K6 [24 sts].
row 26: P2tog to end of row [12 sts].
row 27: K2tog, knit to last 2 sts, K2tog [10 sts].

Neck

Change to flesh-coloured yarn.
rows 28–34: SS for 7 rows.

Head

row 35: knit, inc 1 st at each end [12 sts].
row 36: purl, inc 1 st at each end [14 sts].
row 37: K6, inc 2 sts, K6 [16 sts].
row 38: purl.
row 39: inc 3 sts, K3, inc 4 sts, K3, inc 3 sts [26 sts].
row 40: purl.
row 41: knit, inc 1 st at each end [28 sts].
row 42: purl.
row 43: knit, inc 1 st at each end [30 sts].
rows 44–56: SS for 13 rows.
row 57: K2tog to end of row [15 sts].
row 58: purl.
row 59: K1, then K2tog to end of row [8 sts].
row 60: purl.
row 61: K2tog to end of row [4 sts].
row 62: purl and cast off.

Making up

1. Fold the torso in half, right sides together. Using backstitch, sew from the top of the head down to 1cm (½in) from the top of the neck.
2. Sew up the centre back seam from the bottom upwards until you are 1cm (½in) from the start of the neck.
3. Turn the work right-side out and stuff the top of the head.

Inserting the backbone

1. Take either a piece of dowelling, a roll of cardboard, an unsharpened pencil or a chopstick that is about 1–2cm (½–¾in) shorter than the combined body and head length of the doll.
2. Wrap sticky tape around it, with the sticky side out, so that it is completely covered.
3. Wrap a fine layer of stuffing along the length of the backbone so that all of the sticky surface is covered.
4. Insert the backbone up through the body and into the head of the doll. Once the backbone is in place, add stuffing through the neck opening and into the head. Shape the head with your fingers until it is a nice, even shape. When you are happy with it, mattress stitch the neck closed.
5. Now continue to stuff the body. Shape the shoulders evenly. When you are finished, whip stitch the base of the body closed.

Ears

Make two.

With flesh-coloured yarn and 3mm (US 3) needles, cast on 3 sts, leaving a long tail at each end.

row 1: knit, inc each st [6 sts].
row 2: purl.
row 3: knit, inc 1 st at each end [8 sts].
row 4: purl.
row 5: knit, inc 1 st at each end [10 sts].
row 6: purl and cast off.

Making up the ears

You may find it easier to position the ears once you have created the face.

1. Place both ears in front of you so that one is the mirror image of the other. The longer side is the outer rim of the ear, so have these facing outwards.
2. For both ears, use the left-over tail thread at the bottom of the ear to make small running stitches around the lobe and up the outer rim. Pull the thread firmly so that the ear lobe becomes rounded in shape. Secure with a small stitch, neaten the thread and cut off. Leave the other tail thread and use it to secure the ear to the side of the head. This should make a fairy-like ear, slightly pointed at the top and round at the bottom.
3. Pin the ears to the side of the head, slightly nearer to the back of the head than to the front. Make sure the two ears are level, and align the side of the ear that will be attached to the head with the edge of the nose. Mattress stitch each ear to the head using the spare tail threads.
4. Make a stitch securing the middle of each ear to the head, thus pinning the ears back so they do not stick out. Neaten the threads and cut off the excess.

Arms

Make two.

Using flesh-coloured yarn and 3mm (US 3) needles, cast on 3 sts.

row 1: knit, inc each st [6 sts].
row 2: purl.
row 3: knit, inc 1 st at each end [8 sts].
rows 4–6: SS for 3 rows.
row 7: cast on 3 sts, knit to end [11 sts].
row 8: cast on 3 sts, purl to end [14 sts].
row 9: cast off 3 sts, knit to end [11 sts].
row 10: cast off 3 sts, purl to end [8 sts].
row 11: K2tog, knit to last 2 sts, K2tog [6 sts].
rows 12–40: SS for 29 rows.
row 41: K2tog to end of row [3 sts].
row 42: purl and cast off.

Making up the arms

1. Fold each arm in half lengthwise, wrong sides together, and mattress stitch from the tip of the fingers to 1cm (½in) below the top of the arm. Do not stuff the arms.
2. Pin each arm in place on the body so that the top of each arm is flush with the shoulder. Make sure the arms are evenly placed, then use mattress stitch to sew them in position around the armhole. Neaten the threads and trim them off.

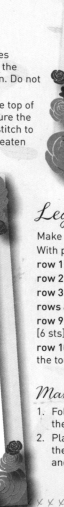

Legs

Make two.

With pink yarn and 3mm (US 3) needles, cast on 3 sts.

row 1: knit, inc in each st [6 sts].
row 2: purl.
row 3: knit, inc in each st [12 sts].
rows 4–8: SS for 5 rows.
row 9: change to flesh-coloured yarn and K2tog to end of row [6 sts].
row 10 onwards: SS until leg measure 23cm (9in) from the tip of the toe and cast off.

Making up the legs

1. Fold the legs, wrong sides together, and mattress stitch from the toe to the top of the leg. Do not stuff the female fairy legs.
2. Place the legs evenly under the base of the body, making sure the leg seam is at the back. Whip stitch the legs on to the body and neaten and trim the threads.

Finishing the body

Needlesculpt the body and head following the instructions on page 9.

Face

See pages 9–10 for needlesculpting the face and making the eyes, nose and lips.

I have embroidered just the tip of Rose Flower Fairy's nose to give her a sweet, innocent appearance. Her eyes are coloured blue for the irises and brown on the lids. I have embroidered on her gently curved eyebrows and a few long eyelashes on the outer edge of each upper eyelid using dark brown embroidery thread. Rose's lips are cut from deep red felt. To finish the face, I have dabbed a little pink colour on to her cheeks and a touch of lilac on to the upper part of the eye socket (see page 11).

Hair

See the general instructions on page 11. Here I have used a variegated eyelash yarn in shades of brown, pink and purple, though any similar fancy yarn will do.

1. Wind the yarn around a large book to obtain the length of hair you want, and cut along one edge.
2. Take each strand in turn, fold it in half and hook it through a single knitted stitch on the fairy's scalp with a crochet hook.
3. Once the head is covered in a good, thick layer of hair, trim the hair to the correct length if desired.

Small petal skirt

Petals

Make three.

Using pink light DK (5-ply/sport) yarn and 3mm (US 3) needles, cast on 4 sts.

row 1: knit, inc each st [8 sts].
row 2: purl.
row 3: knit, inc each st [16 sts].
row 4: purl.
row 5: knit, inc 1 st at each end of row [18 sts].
row 6: purl.
rows 7–10: repeat rows 5 and 6 until 22 sts on needle, ending with a purl row.
row 11: knit, inc 1 st at each end of row [24 sts].
rows 12–16: SS for 5 rows, starting with a purl row.
row 17: K2tog, knit to last 2 sts, K2tog [22 sts].
row 18: purl.
rows 19–24: repeat rows 17 and 18 until 16 sts rem, ending with a purl row.
row 25: K2tog to end of row [8 sts].
row 26: purl and cast off.

Rosebuds

Make two.

With pink yarn and 3mm (US 3) needles, cast on 30 sts.

rows 1–9: SS for 9 rows.
row 10: P2tog to end of row [15 sts].
row 11: K2tog to last st, K1 and cast off on this row.

Assembling the rosebuds

Lay the length of knitting out (it is not necessary to iron it). Start at the corner of one end and begin to roll up the knitting. To avoid making a tube, put pressure on the bottom edge while rolling and let the top 'blossom out' like a rose. When the knitting is rosebud shaped, secure with a couple of stitches and neaten the thread and trim, leaving a long tail.

Making up the small skirt

1. Place the three small petals in a row and stitch them together at the top corners.
2. Neaten all the loose threads. Crochet 2 chains, each 10cm (4in) long, or knit 2 chains using knit 1 st, turn, knit 1 st. Alternatively, use lengths of fine ribbon. Attach a chain to either side of the waist.
3. Stitch the rosebuds to the front of the skirt using the long tail threads. Neaten the threads.

Large petal skirt

Petals

Make three.

Using pink light DK (5-ply/sport) yarn and 3mm (US 3) needles, cast on 4 sts.

row 1: knit, inc each st [8 sts].
row 2: purl
row 3: knit, inc each st [16 sts].
row 4: purl.
row 5: knit, inc each st [32 sts].
row 6: purl.
row 7: knit, inc 1 st at each end of row [34 sts].
row 8: purl.
rows 9–14: repeat rows 7 and 8 until 40 sts on needle, ending with a purl row.
row 15: inc 1 st at each end of row [42 sts].
rows 16–30: SS for 15 rows.
row 31: K2tog, knit to last 2 sts, K2tog [40 sts].
row 32: purl.
rows 33–40: repeat rows 31 and 32 until 32 sts rem, ending with a purl row.
row 41: K2tog to end of row [16 sts].
row 42: purl.
row 43: K2tog to end of row [8 sts].
row 44: purl.
row 45: K2tog to end of row [4 sts].
row 46: purl and cast off.

Making up the large skirt

1. Place the three large petals in a row and stitch them together at the top corners.
2. Neaten all the loose threads. Crochet 2 chains, each 10cm (4in) long, or knit 2 chains using knit 1 st, turn, knit 1 st. Alternatively, use lengths of fine ribbon. Thread five beads on to the end of each chain and secure. Attach a chain to either side of the waist.

Sleeves

Make two small petals following the pattern on page 53. Fold each small petal in half, right sides together, and stitch along their length leaving an opening at either end. Turn right-side out and pull a sleeve over each arm. Stitch the top of each sleeve to the knitted-on bodice, sewing around the 'armhole'.

Wings

Make two (one will form the upper wings and the other the lower wings).

Using the variegated yarn and 4mm (US 6) needles, cast on 3 sts.

row 1: knit, inc each st [6 sts].
row 2: purl.
row 3: knit, inc each st [12 sts].
rows 4–24: SS for 21 rows.
row 25: K2tog to end of row [6 sts].
row 26: purl.
row 27: K2tog to end of row [3 sts].
row 28: purl and cast off.

Making up the wings

1. Neaten all the threads. Place the two wings one on top of the other, right sides facing, and stitch them together using a 1cm (½in) seam along the centre of one edge.
2. Fold out the wings and make a line of running stitch from top to bottom. Pull the thread firmly to gather the knitting into the shape of the wings. Secure and neaten the threads.
2. Wire the wings if desired (see page 9). These wings work well if only the upper wings are wired.
3. Sew on a press-stud, with one half on the top of the wings in the middle and the other in the centre of the fairy's back. Alternatively, sew the wings directly on to the fairy.

To finish the fairy

Make a choker necklace by first threading two large glass beads on to a silver-plated headpin and bending over the top to form a small loop. Thread a variety of beads on to a length of fine wire at least 10cm (4in) long, threading on the headpin about halfway. Wrap the necklace twice around the fairy's neck and secure by twisting the ends together. Snip off or hide the ends.

Tie the fairy's hair up to one side in a high pony tail with a length of beads threaded on to nylon thread.

Alexis the Ice Fairy

Alexis is a majestic fairy. Her queen-like stance and haughty gaze cause the other fairies to flutter away as she glides regally amongst them. Her gentle steps, like softly falling snow, reflect the tender nature of this beautiful fairy, which she hides well beneath her ice-like exterior. Her pale skin, white shimmering hair and snow-white gowns keep her well hidden during the winter months. So next time you hear the gentle sound of snow falling from a bough, or see tiny footsteps in the snow, don't blame the birds or other tiny creatures – it might just have been Alexis passing by.

You will need

All of the items you need to make the
fairies in this book are listed on page 8.
The specific yarns, needles, threads and
embellishments you need to make Alexis are
listed below, though you can, of course, use
suitable alternatives instead, depending on
the style of doll you wish to create and what
materials are available to you.

Yarns:

* ★ Flesh-coloured double-knitting yarn
  (8-ply/light worsted) for body
* ★ Sparkly white yarn for legs and dress
* ★ White eyelash yarn for hair,
  eyelashes, dress and collar
* ★ Cream-coloured 3-ply (light
  fingering) yarn for wings

Needles:

* ★ 3mm (US 3), 7mm (US 11) and 4mm
  (US 6) knitting needles

Threads:

* ★ Dark brown embroidery thread
  for eyebrows

For finishing the fairy:

* ★ Press-stud for fastening the dress; pearl
  and silver beads to decorate dress;
  silver charms for earrings; pearl trim
  for necklace

Torso and head

Using flesh-coloured yarn and 3mm (US 3) needles, cast on 24 sts.
rows 1–10: SS, ending with a purl row.

Waist

row 11: K2tog, K5, K2tog, K6, K2tog, K5, K2tog [20 sts].
rows 12–14: SS for 3 rows.
row 15: inc 1 st, K5, inc 1 st, K6, inc 1 st, K5, inc 1 st [24 sts].
rows 16–22: SS for 7 rows.

Shoulders

row 23: K6, inc 2 sts, K8, inc 2 sts, K6 [28 sts].
row 24: purl.
row 25: K6, K2tog twice, K8, K2tog twice, K6 [24 sts].
row 26: P2tog to end of row [12 sts].
row 27: K2tog, knit to last 2 sts, K2tog [10 sts].

Neck

rows 28–34: SS for 7 rows.

Head

row 35: knit, inc 1 st at each end [12 sts].
row 36: purl, inc 1 st at each end [14 sts].
row 37: K6, inc 2 sts, K6 [16 sts].
row 38: purl.
row 39: inc 3 sts, K3, inc 4 sts, K3, inc 3 sts [26 sts].
row 40: purl.
row 41: knit, inc 1 st at each end [28 sts].
row 42: purl.
row 43: knit, inc 1 st at each end [30 sts].
rows 44–56: SS for 13 rows.
row 57: K2tog to end of row [15 sts].
row 58: purl.
row 59: K1, then K2tog to end of row [8 sts].
row 60: purl.
row 61: K2tog to end of row [4 sts].
row 62: purl and cast off.

Making up

1. Fold the torso in half, right sides together. Using backstitch, sew from the top of the head down to 1cm (½in) from the top of the neck.

2. Sew up the centre back seam from the bottom upwards until you are 1cm (½in) from the start of the neck.
3. Turn the work right-side out and stuff the top of the head.

Inserting the backbone

1. Take either a piece of dowelling, a roll of cardboard, an unsharpened pencil or a chopstick that is about 1–2cm (½–¾in) shorter than the combined body and head length of the doll.
2. Wrap sticky tape around it, with the sticky side out, so that it is completely covered.
3. Wrap a fine layer of stuffing along the length of the backbone so that all of the sticky surface is covered.
4. Insert the backbone up through the body and into the head of the doll. Once the backbone is in place, add stuffing through the neck opening and into the head. Shape the head with your fingers until it is a nice, even shape. When you are happy with it, mattress stitch the neck closed.
5. Now continue to stuff the body. Shape the shoulders evenly. When you are finished, whip stitch the base of the body closed.

Ears

Make two.

Using flesh-coloured yarn and 3mm (US 3) needles, cast on 3 sts, leaving a long tail at each end.

row 1: knit, inc each st [6 sts].

row 2: purl.

row 3: knit, inc 1 st at each end [8 sts].

row 4: purl.

row 5: knit, inc 1 st at each end [10 sts].

row 6: purl and cast off.

Making up the ears

You may find it easier to position the ears once you have created the face.

1. Place both ears in front of you so that one is the mirror image of the other. The longer side is the outer rim of the ear, so have these facing outwards.

2. For both ears, use the left-over tail thread at the bottom of the ear to make small running stitches around the lobe and up the outer rim. Pull the thread firmly so that the ear lobe becomes rounded in shape. Secure with a small stitch, neaten the thread and cut off. Leave the other tail thread and use it to secure the ear to the side of the head. This should make a fairy-like ear, slightly pointed at the top and round at the bottom.

3. Pin the ears to the side of the head, slightly nearer to the back of the head than to the front. Ensure the ears are level, and align the side of the ear attached to the head with the edge of the nose. Mattress stitch each ear to the head using the spare tail threads.

4. Make a stitch securing the middle of each ear to the head, thus pinning the ears back so they do not stick out. Neaten the threads and cut off the excess.

Arms

Make two.

Using flesh-coloured yarn and 3mm (US 3) needles, cast on 3 sts.

row 1: knit, inc each st [6 sts].

row 2: purl.

row 3: knit, inc 1 st at each end [8 sts].

rows 4–6: SS for 3 rows.

row 7: cast on 3 sts, knit to end [11 sts].

row 8: cast on 3 sts, purl to end [14 sts].

row 9: cast off 3 sts, knit to end [11 sts].

row 10: cast off 3 sts, purl to end [8 sts].

row 11: K2tog, knit to last 2 sts, K2tog [6 sts].

rows 12–40: SS for 29 rows.

row 41: K2tog to end of row [3 sts].

row 42: purl and cast off.

Making up the arms

1. Fold each arm in half lengthwise, wrong sides together, and mattress stitch from the tip of the fingers to 1cm (½in) below the top of the arm. Do not stuff the arms.
2. Pin each arm in place on the body so that the top of each arm is flush with the shoulder. Make sure the arms are evenly placed, then use mattress stitch to sew them in position around the armhole. Neaten the threads and trim them off.

Legs

Make two.
Using sparkly white yarn and 3mm (US 3) needles, cast on 3 sts.
row 1: knit, inc each st [6 sts].
row 2: purl.
row 3: knit, inc 1 st at each end [8 sts].
row 4: purl.
row 5: knit, inc 1 st at each end [10 sts].
row 6: purl.
row 7: knit, inc 1 st at each end [12 sts].
rows 8–12: SS for 5 rows, starting with a purl row.
row 13: K2tog twice, K4, K2tog twice [8 sts].
row 14: purl.
row 15: K2tog, knit to last 2 sts, K2tog [6 sts].
rows 16–31: SS for 16 rows.
rows 32–36: introduce the white eyelash yarn and GS for 5 rows.
rows 37–62: change back to white yarn and continue in SS. Cast off on last purl row.

Making up the legs

1. Fold the legs, wrong sides together, and mattress stitch from the toe to the top of the leg. Do not stuff the female fairy legs.
2. Place the legs evenly under the base of the body, making sure the leg seam is at the back. Whip stitch the legs on to the body and neaten and trim the threads.

Finishing the body

Needlesculpt the body and head following the instructions on page 9.

Face

See pages 9–10 for needlesculpting the face and making the eyes, nose and lips.

Alexis' nose is embroidered from the tip up to her eyes. Her eyes are coloured blue for the irises and brown on the lids. Her rather stern eyebrows are embroidered on in a straight, diagonal line and her lips are cut from deep red felt. To finish the face, I have dabbed a little pink colour on to Alexis' cheeks and placed a touch of light blue on to the upper part of the eye socket and down either side of her nose (see page 11).

Eyelashes

Cut a short length of white eyelash yarn, about 2cm (¾in) long. Cut it in half and trim each half at an angle so that the eyelashes are shorter at one end than the other. Measure each length of eyelashes against the eyelid and trim to size. Glue each one in place, ensuring the eyelashes are longer on the outside than at the inner eye.

Hair

1. Wind a length of white eyelash yarn around five fingers until it forms a soft ball. Cut off the yarn and stitch the ball to the fairy's head to form a soft, loose covering of hair.
2. For the longer sections of her hair, wind yarn around a large book to obtain the length of hair required. Cut through the loops along one edge. Fold the strands in half and stitch them firmly on to the fairy's head, near the front. Tie the long hair up high on her head for a more regal appearance.

Dress

Skirt

Using sparkly white yarn and 4mm (US 6) needles cast on 120 sts.

rows 1–26: SS for 26 rows.
row 27: K2tog to end of row [60 sts].
row 28: purl.
row 29: change to white eyelash yarn and use 7mm (US 11) needles to knit row.
rows 30–38: GS for 9 rows.
row 39: change back to 4mm (US 6) needles and K2tog to end of row [30 sts].
row 40: knit.
row 41: *K1, K2tog*, repeat from * to * to end of row [20 sts].
row 42: knit and cast off.

Bodice

With sparkly white yarn and 4mm (US 6) needles, cast on 22 sts.

rows 1–10: SS for 10 rows. Cast off on last row.

Collar

Using eyelash yarn and 4mm (US 6) needles, cast on 5 sts.
rows 1–45: GS, casting off on the last row.

Making up the dress

1. Fold the skirt in half, right sides together, and backstitch the centre back seam leaving a 1cm (½in) opening at the waist. Neaten all the loose threads and sew a press-stud on to either side of the waist opening.
2. Fold the bodice in half right sides together and backstitch the seam from top to bottom. Neaten any loose threads. Turn the bodice right-side out and pull it up over the fairy's torso. Pull the skirt on up to the bodice with the opening at the back. Sew the skirt to the bodice. Finish the skirt by sewing on pearl and silver beads.
3. Sew one half of a press-stud on to each end of the collar, one on the top of the knitting and one on the bottom. When secured, one end of the collar should overlap the other. Stitch the middle of the collar to the centre front of the bodice.

Wings

Right wing

Using cream-coloured 3-ply (light fingering) yarn and 4mm (US 6) needles, cast on 5 sts.
row 1: knit, inc 1 st at each end [7 sts].
row 2: purl.
rows 3–10: repeat rows 1 and 2 until 15 sts on needle, ending with a purl row.
rows 11–14: SS for 4 rows.
row 15: K2tog, knit to last 2 sts, K2tog [13 sts].
row 16: purl.
rows 17–20: repeat rows 15 and 16 until 9 sts rem, ending with a purl row.
row 21: knit, inc 1 st at each end [11 sts].
row 22: cast on 2 sts, purl to end [13 sts].
row 23: knit, inc 1 st at each end [15 sts].
row 24: purl.

rows 25–28: repeat rows 23 and 24 until 19 sts on needle, ending with a purl row.

rows 29–32: SS for 4 rows.

row 33: knit to last st, inc 1 st [20 sts].

row 34: purl.

rows 35–38: repeat rows 33 and 34 until 22 sts on needle.

rows 39–42: SS for 4 rows.

row 43: K2tog, knit to last st, inc 1 st [22 sts].

row 44: purl.

rows 45–52: repeat rows 43 and 44 four times.

row 53: K2tog, knit to last 2 sts, K2tog [20 sts].

row 54: purl.

rows 55–64: repeat rows 53 and 54 until 10 sts rem, ending with a purl row.

row 65: K2tog twice, K2, K2tog twice [6 sts].

row 66: purl.

row 67: K2tog, K2, K2tog [4 sts].

row 68: purl and cast off.

Left wing

Work as for right wing until row 22.

row 22: purl.

row 23: cast on 2 sts, knit to end [13 sts].

row 24: purl.

row 25: knit, inc 1 st at each end [15 sts].

row 26: purl.

rows 27–30: repeat rows 25 and 26 until 19 sts on needle, ending with a purl row.

rows 31–34: SS for 4 rows.

row 35: inc 1 st, knit to end [20 sts].

row 36: purl.

rows 37–40: repeat rows 35 and 36 until 22 sts on needle.

rows 41–44: SS for 4 rows.

row 45: inc 1 st, knit to last 2 sts, K2tog [22 sts].

row 46: purl.

rows 47–54: repeat rows 45 and 46.

row 55: K2tog, knit to last 2 sts, K2tog [20 sts].

row 56: purl.

rows 57–66: repeat rows 55 and 56 until 10 sts rem, ending with a purl row.

row 67: K2tog twice, K2, K2tog twice [6 sts].

row 68: purl.

row 69: K2tog, K2, K2tog [4 sts].

row 70: purl and cast off.

Making up the wings

1. Place the wings with right sides together. Stitch the two pieces together in the middle with a 1–2cm (½–¾in) seam.

2. Bend 2 chenille sticks or lengths of fine floristry wire into the shape of the outstretched wings. Stitch the wire to the back of the wings with mattress stitch.

3. Wind a third chenille stick around the middle of the wings, where they join, and bend the two ends into loops on the right side of the knitting. These should be large enough to fit comfortably but snugly over the fairy's arms to hold the wings in place. Alternatively, sew one half of a press-stud on to the front of the wings in the centre and the other half on to the middle of the fairy's back. You may also stitch the wings directly on to the fairy if they do not need to be removable.

To finish the fairy

Thread silver charms through each of her earlobes using white sewing thread for earrings, and wind a length of pearl trim around her neck for a necklace. Secure it at the back.

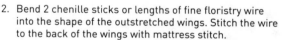

Blossom Tree Fairy

Spring is a celebration of life – the sun awakens after the winter's cold, breathing new life into the myriad of plants and animals that inhabit the earth. Pink and white blossom bursts from the boughs of fruit trees, and the countryside is cloaked once more in a mantle of green, fresh and bright. This is the season that Blossom Tree Fairy loves the most. Clothed in bright pinks and greens, trimmed with blossom flowers and butterflies, he dances happily in the fields and gardens, heralding the birth of another year.

You will need

All of the items you need to make the fairies in this book are listed on page 8. The specific yarns, needles, threads and embellishments you need to make Blossom Tree Fairy are listed below, though you can, of course, use suitable alternatives instead, depending on the style of doll you wish to create and what materials are available to you.

Yarns:

★ Flesh-coloured and variegated pink and green double-knitting yarn (8-ply/light worsted) for body
★ Turquoise, brown and red double-knitting yarn (8-ply/light worsted) for legs
★ Pale green fluffy yarn or fine feather boa for hair and collar
★ Bright green double-knitting yarn (8-ply/light worsted) for pantaloons and hat
★ Dark green light DK (5-ply/sport) yarn for wings

Needles:

★ 3mm (US 3), 7mm (US 11) and 4mm (US 6) knitting needles

Threads:

★ Brown embroidery thread for eyebrows

For finishing the fairy:

★ Press-stud for fastening the pantaloons; silk blossoms to decorate hat and boots; coloured butterfly charms to decorate hat and pantaloons; green chenille sticks for wiring the wings (if desired)

Torso and head

Using variegated pink and green yarn and 3mm (US 3) needles, cast on 24 sts.
rows 1–10: SS, ending with a purl row.

Waist

row 11: K2tog, K5, K2tog, K6, K2tog, K5, K2tog [20 sts].
rows 12–14: SS for 3 rows.
row 15: knit, inc 1 st, K5, inc 1 st, K6, inc 1 st, K5, inc 1 st [24 sts].
rows 16–22: SS for 7 rows.

Shoulders

row 23: K6, inc 2 sts, K8, inc 2 sts, K6 [28 sts].
row 24: purl.
row 25: K6, K2tog twice, K8, K2tog twice, K6 [24 sts].
row 26: P2tog to end of row [12 sts].
row 27: change to flesh-coloured yarn, then K2tog, knit to last 2 sts, K2tog [10 sts].

Neck

rows 28–34: SS for 7 rows.

Head

row 35: knit, inc 1 st at each end [12 sts].
row 36: purl, inc 1 st at each end [14 sts].
row 37: K6, inc 2 sts, K6 [16 sts].
row 38: purl.
row 39: knit, inc 3 sts, K3, inc 4 sts, K3, inc 3 sts [26 sts].
row 40: purl.
row 41: knit, inc 1 st at each end [28 sts].
row 42: purl.
row 43: knit, inc 1 st at each end [30 sts].
rows 44–56: SS for 13 rows.
row 57: K2tog to end of row [15 sts].
row 58: purl.
row 59: K1, then K2tog to end of row [8 sts].
row 60: purl.
row 61: K2tog to end of row [4 sts].
row 62: purl and cast off.

Making up

1. Fold the torso in half, right sides together. Using backstitch, sew from the top of the head down to 1cm (½in) from the top of the neck.

2. Sew up the centre back seam from the bottom upwards until you are 1cm (½in) from the start of the neck.
3. Turn right-side out and stuff the top of the head.

Inserting the backbone

1. Take either a piece of dowelling, a roll of cardboard, an unsharpened pencil or a chopstick that is about 1–2cm (½–¾in) shorter than the combined body and head length of the doll.
2. Wrap sticky tape around it, with the sticky side out, so that it is completely covered.
3. Wrap a fine layer of stuffing along the length of the backbone so that all of the sticky surface is covered.
4. Insert the backbone up through the body and into the head of the doll. Once the backbone is in place, add stuffing through the neck opening and into the head. Shape the head with your fingers until it is a nice, even shape. When you are happy with it, mattress stitch the neck closed.
5. Now continue to stuff the body. Shape the shoulders evenly. When you are finished, whip stitch the base of the body closed.

Ears

Make two.

With flesh-coloured yarn and 3mm (US 3) needles, cast on 3 sts, leaving a long tail at each end.

row 1: knit, inc each st [6 sts].

row 2: purl.

row 3: knit, inc 1 st at each end [8 sts].

row 4: purl.

row 5: knit, inc 1 st at each end [10 sts].

row 6: purl and cast off.

Making up the ears

You may find it easier to position the ears once you have created the face.

1. Place both ears in front of you so that one is the mirror image of the other. The longer side is the outer rim of the ear, so have these facing outwards.

2. For both ears, use the left-over tail thread at the bottom of the ear to make small running stitches around the lobe and up the outer rim. Pull the thread firmly so that the ear lobe becomes rounded in shape. Secure with a small stitch, neaten the thread and cut off. Leave the other tail thread and use it to secure the ear to the side of the head. This should make a fairy-like ear, slightly pointed at the top and round at the bottom.

3. Pin the ears to the side of the head, slightly nearer to the back of the head than to the front. Make sure the two ears are level, and align the side of the ear attached to the head with the edge of the nose. Mattress stitch each ear to the head using the spare tail threads.

4. Make a stitch securing the middle of each ear to the head, thus pinning the ears back so they do not stick out. Neaten the threads and cut off the excess.

Arms

Make two.

Using flesh-coloured yarn and 3mm (US 3) needles, cast on 3 sts.

row 1: knit, inc each st [6 sts].

row 2: purl.

row 3: knit, inc 1 st at each end [8 sts].

rows 4–6: SS for 3 rows.

row 7: cast on 3 sts, knit to end [11 sts].

row 8: cast on 3 sts, purl to end [14 sts].

row 9: cast off 3 sts, knit to end [11 sts].

row 10: cast off 3 sts, purl to end [8 sts].

row 11: K2tog, knit to last 2 sts, K2tog [6 sts].

rows 12–40: SS for 29 rows, changing to variegated yarn at row 15.

row 41: K2tog to end of row [3 sts].

row 42: purl and cast off.

Making up the arms

1. Fold each arm in half lengthwise, wrong sides together, and mattress stitch from the tip of the fingers to 1cm (½in) below the top of the arm. Do not stuff the arms.

2. Pin each arm in place on the body so that the top of each arm is flush with the shoulder. Make sure the arms are evenly placed, then use mattress stitch to sew them in position around the armhole. Neaten the threads and trim them off.

Legs

Make two.

With turquoise yarn and 3mm (US 3) needles, cast on 3 sts.

rows 1-8: SS for 8 rows.

row 9: knit, inc 1 st at each end [5 sts].

row 10: purl.

row 11: knit, inc 1 st at each end [7 sts].

row 12: purl.

row 13: knit, inc 1 st at each end [9 sts].

row 14: purl.

row 15: knit, inc 1 st at each end [11 sts].

row 16: purl.

Finishing the body

Needlesculpt the body and head following the instructions on page 9.

Face

See pages 9–10 for needlesculpting the face and making the eyes, nose and lips.

Blossom Tree Fairy has a small, embroidered button nose and his eyes are coloured using blue for the irises and brown on the lids. His straight eyebrows are angled sharply, giving him a rather mischievous appearance, and are embroidered using brown thread. His red lips are cut from bright red felt, and I have coloured his cheeks and the tip of his nose quite heavily with pink. Around his eyes I have used smudges of grey-green (see page 11).

Hair

Cut a small length of pale green fluffy yarn or trim, such as fine feather boa, and coil it around on the top of the fairy's head. Once it is arranged as you'd like it, pin it in place. Stitch the hair to the scalp with a needle and sewing thread.

row 17: knit, inc 1 st at each end [13 sts].
rows 18–20: SS for 3 rows.
row 21: cast on 3 sts, knit to end [16 sts].
row 22: cast on 3 sts, purl to end [19 sts].
rows 23–26: SS for 4 rows.
row 27: cast off 4 sts, knit to end [15 sts].
row 28: cast off 4 sts, purl to end [11 sts].
row 29: K2tog, knit to last 2 sts, K2tog [9 sts].
rows 30–44: SS for 15 rows.
rows 45–73: change to brown yarn and do a further 29 rows of SS, changing to red yarn on every alternate row. Cast off on the last row.

Making up the legs

1. Fold the legs, wrong sides together, and mattress stitch from the toe to the top of the leg. Stuff the legs firmly but don't over stuff.
2. Place the legs evenly under the base of the body, making sure the leg seam is at the back. Whip stitch the legs on to the body and neaten and trim the threads. Wrap a thread tightly around each leg, just above the top of the boot, and fasten off.
3. For each boot, secure a thread at the tip of the toe and make small running stitches along the back seam to the top of the boot. Pull the thread firmly to make the toe of the boot curl. Secure and neaten the thread.

Pantaloons

Make two.

Using bright green yarn and 4mm (US 6) needles, cast on 12 sts.

row 1: knit, inc each st [24 sts].

row 2: purl.

row 3: knit, inc 1 st at each end [26 sts].

row 4: purl.

row 5: knit, inc 1 st at each end [28 sts].

row 6: purl.

row 7: knit, inc 1 st at each end [30 sts].

rows 8–22: SS for 15 rows.

row 23: K2tog, knit to last 2 sts, K2tog [28 sts].

row 24: purl.

row 25: K6, K2tog, K3, K2tog, K2, K2tog, K3, K2tog, K6 [24 sts].

row 26: purl.

row 27: K2tog to end of row [12 sts].

row 28: purl and cast off.

Making up the pantaloons

1. Place the two pieces of knitting with right sides together. On each side of the knitting, backstitch down from the waist to the crotch. On one side, leave a 1cm (½in) opening at the waist.

2. Unfold the pants and refold them so that the two seams are now in the middle, one on top of the other (still with right sides together). Backstitch from one leg opening, across the crotch and down to the other leg opening. Neaten the threads and turn right-side out.

3. Sew on a press-stud to secure the opening at the waist. Sew butterfly charms around the waistband.

Hat

Using bright green yarn and 4mm (US 6) needles, cast on 3 sts.

row 1: knit, inc each st [6 sts].

row 2: purl.

row 3: knit, inc each st [12 sts].

row 4: purl.

row 5: knit, inc each st [24 sts].

row 6: purl.

row 7: knit, inc each st [48 sts].

rows 8–12: SS for 5 rows.

row 13: knit, inc 1 st at each end [50 sts].

row 14: purl.

row 15: knit 5 sts, turn and work on these sts only.

row 16: purl.

row 17: knit.

row 18: purl.

row 19: K2tog, K1, K2tog [3 sts].

row 20: purl.

row 21: K2tog and cast off.

Repeat rows 15–21 nine times to make the edging around the rim of the hat.

Making up the hat

1. Backstitch along the centre back seam from the middle of the hat to the rim. Turn right-side out. Work running stitches around the brim, just before the start of the petals. Pull the thread firmly to fit the head snugly and secure. Neaten all the threads.

2. Sew a butterfly charm on to each petal of the brim, and stitch silk blossom over the top of the hat to decorate.

Wings

Make two.

Using light DK (5-ply/sport) silky green yarn and 4mm (US 6) needles, cast on 3 sts.

row 1: knit, inc each st [6 sts].
row 2: purl.
row 3: knit, inc 1 st at each end [8 sts].
row 4: purl.
rows 5–18: repeat rows 3 and 4 until 22 sts on needle, ending with a purl row.
rows 19–22: SS for 4 rows.
row 23: K2tog, knit to last 2 sts, K2tog [20 sts].
row 24: purl.
rows 25–40: repeat rows 23 and 24 until 4 sts rem, ending with a purl row.
row 41: K2tog twice [2 sts].
row 42: purl.
row 43: K2tog and cast off.

Making up the wings

1. Lay the wings out flat, right sides down, and bend a long, green chenille stick into the shape of each wing. Use ladder stitch to secure each chenille stick around the edge of a wing, leaving about 10cm (4in) spare at each end. Stitch on the back of the knitting, so that the stitching doesn't show on the front.

2. Put the wings side by side, right sides up, with the ends of the chenille sticks in the middle. Twist the chenille sticks together and form them into armhole loops to fit comfortably over each of the fairy's arms.

3. If you prefer not to wire the wings, stitch them together in the middle and attach them to the fairy either using a press-stud or by sewing them on.

To finish the fairy

Make a fluffy collar by stitching a short length of the same trim that you used for his hair around his neck and trimming off the excess. Attach a silk blossom to the front of each boot.

Lily Water Fairy

Ponds, lakes, streams and rivers are the home of
Lily Water Fairy. Hiding amongst the reeds and the
bullrushes, dancing with the dragonflies and riding
on the backs of toads are amongst her favourite
pastimes. Her long, wavy brown hair resembles water
weed as she swims through the water. Her clothes
of green and blue disguise her well, and her slender
form may often be mistaken for a fish or a frog as she
dives and frolics in the water. So next time you catch
a shimmer and a splash out of the corner of your eye,
perhaps it is Lily Water Fairy.

You will need

All of the items you need to make the fairies in this book are listed on page 8. The specific yarns, needles, threads and embellishments you need to make Lily Water Fairy are listed below, though you can, of course, use suitable alternatives instead, depending on the style of doll you wish to create and what materials are available to you.

Yarns:

* Blue and flesh-coloured double-knitting yarn (8-ply/light worsted) for body
* Brown mohair yarn (knitted up and unravelled) for hair
* Variegated eyelash yarn in blues, greens and purples for skirt trims
* Light green light DK (5-ply/sport) yarn for dress
* Variegated light DK (5-ply/sport) yarn in blues, greens and purples for overskirt and wings

Needles:

* 3mm (US 3), 7mm (US 11) and 4mm (US 6) knitting needles

Threads:

* Dark brown embroidery thread for eyebrows and eyelashes

For finishing the fairy:

* About ten coloured beads for decorating wing tips; three blue cubic beads for front of dress and earrings; small blue beads and fine nylon thread for bracelet; pearl trim for straps of dress

Torso and head

Using flesh-coloured yarn and 3mm (US 3) needles, cast on 24 sts.
rows 1–10: SS, ending with a purl row.

Waist

row 11: K2tog, K5, K2tog, K6, K2tog, K5, K2tog [20 sts].
rows 12–14: SS for 3 rows.
row 15: inc 1 st, K5, inc 1 st, K6, inc 1 st, K5, inc 1 st [24 sts].
rows 16–22: SS for 7 rows.

Shoulders

row 23: K6, inc 2 sts, K8, inc 2 sts, K6 [28 sts].
row 24: purl.
row 25: K6, K2tog twice, K8, K2tog twice, K6 [24 sts].
row 26: P2tog to end of row [12 sts].
row 27: K2tog, knit to last 2 sts, K2tog [10 sts].

Neck

rows 28–34: SS for 7 rows.

Head

row 35: knit, inc 1 st at each end [12 sts].
row 36: purl, inc 1 st at each end [14 sts].
row 37: K6, inc 2 sts, K6 [16 sts].
row 38: purl.
row 39: inc 3 sts, K3, inc 4 sts, K3, inc 3 sts [26 sts].
row 40: purl.
row 41: knit, inc 1 st at each end [28 sts].
row 42: purl.
row 43: knit, inc 1 st at each end [30 sts].
rows 44–56: SS for 13 rows.
row 57: K2tog to end of row [15 sts].
row 58: purl.
row 59: K1, then K2tog to end of row [8 sts].
row 60: purl.
row 61: K2tog to end of row [4 sts].
row 62: purl and cast off.

Making up

1. Fold the torso in half, right sides together. Using backstitch, sew from the top of the head down to 1cm (½in) from the top of the neck.
2. Sew up the centre back seam from the bottom upwards until you are 1cm (½in) from the start of the neck.
3. Turn the work right-side out and stuff the top of the head.

Inserting the backbone

1. Take either a piece of dowelling, a roll of cardboard, an unsharpened pencil or a chopstick that is about 1–2cm (½–¾in) shorter than the combined body and head length of the doll.
2. Wrap sticky tape around it, with the sticky side out, so that it is completely covered.
3. Wrap a fine layer of stuffing along the length of the backbone so that all of the sticky surface is covered.
4. Insert the backbone up through the body and into the head of the doll. Once the backbone is in place, add stuffing through the neck opening and into the head. Shape the head with your fingers until it is a nice, even shape. When you are happy with it, mattress stitch the neck closed.
5. Now continue to stuff the body. Shape the shoulders evenly. When you are finished, whip stitch the base of the body closed.

Ears

Make two.
Using flesh-coloured yarn and 3mm (US 3) needles, cast on 3 sts, leaving a long tail at each end.
row 1: knit, inc each st [6 sts].
row 2: purl.
row 3: knit, inc 1 st at each end [8 sts].
row 4: purl.
row 5: knit, inc 1 st at each end [10 sts].
row 6: purl and cast off.

Making up the ears

You may find it easier to position the ears once you have created the face.

1. Place both ears in front of you so that one is the mirror image of the other. The longer side is the outer rim of the ear, so have these facing outwards.
2. For both ears, use the left-over tail thread at the bottom of the ear to make small running stitches around the lobe and up the outer rim. Pull the thread firmly so that the ear lobe becomes rounded in shape. Secure with a small stitch, neaten the thread and cut off. Leave the other tail thread and use it to secure the ear to the side of the head. This should make a fairy-like ear, slightly pointed at the top and round at the bottom.
3. Pin the ears to the side of the head, slightly nearer to the back of the head than to the front. Make sure the two ears are level, and align the side of the ear that will be attached to the head with the edge of the nose. Mattress stitch each ear to the head using the spare tail threads.
4. Make a stitch securing the middle of each ear to the head, thus pinning the ears back so they do not stick out. Neaten the threads and cut off the excess.

Arms

Make two.
Using flesh-coloured yarn and 3mm (US 3) needles, cast on 3 sts.
row 1: knit, inc each st [6 sts].
row 2: purl.
row 3: knit, inc 1 st at each end [8 sts].
rows 4–6: SS for 3 rows.
row 7: cast on 3 sts, knit to end [11 sts].
row 8: cast on 3 sts, purl to end [14 sts].
row 9: cast off 3 sts, knit to end [11 sts].
row 10: cast off 3 sts, purl to end [8 sts].
row 11: K2tog, knit to last 2 sts, K2tog [6 sts].
rows 12–40: SS for 29 rows.
row 41: K2tog to end of row [3 sts].
row 42: purl and cast off.

Making up the arms

1. Fold each arm in half lengthwise, wrong sides together, and mattress stitch from the tip of the fingers to 1cm (½in) below the top of the arm. Do not stuff the arms.
2. Pin each arm in place on the body so that the top of each arm is flush with the shoulder. Make sure the arms are evenly placed, then use mattress stitch to sew them in position around the armhole. Neaten the threads and trim them off.

Legs

With blue yarn and 3mm (US 3) needles, cast on 3 sts.
row 1: knit, inc each st [6 sts].
row 2: purl.
row 3: knit, inc each st [12 sts].
rows 4–8: SS for 5 rows.
row 9: change to flesh-coloured yarn and K2tog to end [6 sts].
row 10 onwards: SS until leg measures 23cm (9in) from the tip of the toe and cast off.

Making up the legs

1. Fold the legs, wrong sides together, and mattress stitch from the toe to the top of the leg. Do not stuff the female fairy legs.
2. Place the legs evenly under the base of the body, making sure the leg seam is at the back. Whip stitch the legs on to the body and neaten and trim the threads.

Finishing the body

Needlesculpt the body and head following the instructions on page 9.

Face

See pages 9–10 for needlesculpting the face and making the eyes, nose and lips.

I have embroidered the tip of Lily Water Fairy's nose with a broad row of vertical straight stitches, then made the bridge of her nose narrower using horizontal stitching. Her irises and eyelids are both coloured brown. I have embroidered on her gently curved eyebrows and a few long eyelashes on the outer edge of each upper eyelid using fairly thick, dark brown embroidery thread. Lily's lips are cut from deep red felt. To finish the face, I have dabbed a little pink colour on to her cheeks and a touch of light green on to the upper part of the eye socket (see page 11).

Hair

See the general instructions on page 11. Here I have used a brown mohair yarn, which I knitted up, left for a few days and then unravelled. This produced a delightful kink in the strands, which is perfect for Lily's long, wavy hair.

1. Wind the yarn around a large book to obtain the length of hair you want, and cut along one edge.
2. Take each strand in turn, fold it in half and hook it through a single knitted stitch on the fairy's scalp with a crochet hook.
3. Once the head is covered in a good, thick layer of hair, trim the hair to the correct length if desired.
4. As a final touch, I plaited Lily's hair loosely, one or two times, so it sits in a dense ponytail high on her head.

Dress

Using variegated eyelash yarn and 7mm (US 11) needles, cast on 80 sts.

rows 1–4: GS for 4 rows.
row 5: change to light green light DK (5-ply/sport) yarn and purl.
row 6: K2tog to end of row [40 sts].
rows 7–21: SS for 15 rows.
rows 22–25: change to 3mm (US 3) needles and SS for 4 rows.
row 26: K2, K2tog to last 2 sts, K2 [22 sts].
rows 27–31: SS for 5 rows. Cast off on last row.

Making up the dress

1. Fold the dress in half, right sides together. Backstitch up the centre back seam, leaving a 1cm (½in) opening at the top of the bodice and attaching a press-stud. Alternatively, you may be able to pull the dress on to the fairy with the back seam stitched all the way up to the top.
2. Neaten all the threads and turn right-side out. Sew on a short length of pearl trim, attaching the middle of the trim to the centre front of the bodice, taking it over each shoulder and securing both ends in the middle at the back.
3. Sew a blue cubic bead on the front of the dress.

Overskirt

Using variegated eyelash yarn and 7mm (US 11) needles, cast on 52 sts.

rows 1–5: GS for 5 rows.
row 6: K2tog to end of row [26 sts].
row 7: purl.
rows 8–17: change to light DK (5-ply/sport) variegated yarn and SS for 10 rows.
rows 18–21: change to 3mm (US 3) needles and SS for 4 rows.
row 22: K2tog to end of row [13 sts].
rows 23–25: SS for 3 rows, casting off on last row.

Making up the overskirt

Neaten all the loose threads. Place the overskirt over the dress, aligning the waists with the opening at the front. Stitch them together along the waists.

Upper wings

Make one.
Using light DK (5-ply/sport) variegated yarn and 3mm (US 3) needles, cast on 3 sts.

row 1: knit, inc each st [6 sts].
row 2: purl.
row 3: knit, inc each st [12 sts].
row 4: purl.

row 5: knit, inc each st [24 sts].

row 6: purl.

row 7: knit, inc each st [48 sts].

rows 8–18: SS for 11 rows.

row 19: K23, cast off 2 sts, knit to end.

row 20: P23, turn and work on these 23 sts only.

row 21: knit, inc 1 st at each end [25 sts].

row 22: purl.

rows 23–30: repeat rows 21 and 22 until 33 sts on needle, ending with a purl row.

rows 31–35: SS for 5 rows.

row 36: K2tog 8 times, K1, K2tog 8 times [17 sts].

row 37: purl.

row 38: K2tog 4 times, K1, K2tog 4 times [9 sts].

rows 39–47: SS for 9 rows.

row 48: K2tog twice, K1, K2tog twice [5 sts].

rows 49–53: SS for 5 rows.

row 54: K2tog, K1, K2tog [3 sts].

rows 55–59: SS for 5 rows.

row 60: K3tog and cast off.

Go back to remaining 23 sts and repeat rows 20–60.

Lower wings

Make one.

Using light DK (5-ply/sport) variegated yarn and 3mm (US 3) needles, cast on 3 sts.

row 1: knit, inc each st [6 sts].

row 2: purl.

row 3: knit, inc each st [12 sts].

row 4: purl.

row 5: knit, inc each st [24 sts].

row 6: purl.

row 7: *K1, inc 1 st*, repeat from * to * to end of row [36 sts].

row 8: purl.

row 9: K18, cast off 2 sts, knit to end.

row 10: P16, turn and work on these 16 sts only.

row 11: knit, inc 1 st at each end [18 sts].

row 12: purl.

rows 13–24: repeat rows 11 and 12 until 24 sts on needle, ending with a purl row.

rows 25–28: SS for 4 rows.

row 29: K2tog to end of row [12 sts].

row 30: purl.

row 31: K2tog to end of row [6 sts].

rows 32–36: SS for 5 rows.

row 37: K2tog to end of row [3 sts].

rows 38–42: SS for 5 rows.

row 43: K3tog and cast off, leaving a long tail thread of about 20cm (8in) long.

Go back to remaining 18 sts and repeat rows 10–43.

Making up the wings

1. Place the two wings together with right sides facing. Stitch them together in the middle, making a seam about 1–2cm (½–¾in) long.

2. Run a line of running stitches across the centre of the outspread wings and pull the thread firmly to gather. This will turn the two wing pieces into four wings – two upper and two lower. Wire the wings, if desired (see page 9).

3. Neaten all the loose threads. Knit a 5cm (2in) chain using knit 1 st, turn, knit 1 st, on to the tip of each upper wing.

4. Thread five metallic beads on to the tail thread of each lower wing, then use the rest of the tail thread to knit a 5cm (2in) chain, as in step 3.

3. Attach the wings to the fairy with a press-stud, one half sewn on to the right side of the wings in the middle and the other half sewn on to the centre of the fairy's back. Alternatively, sew the wings directly on to her body.

To finish the fairy

Attach a blue glass bead, to match the glass bead on the front of her dress, to each earlobe, and make a bracelet using smaller versions of the blue beads threaded on to a length of fine nylon thread. Tie the string of beads into a circle and slip it on to the fairy's wrist.

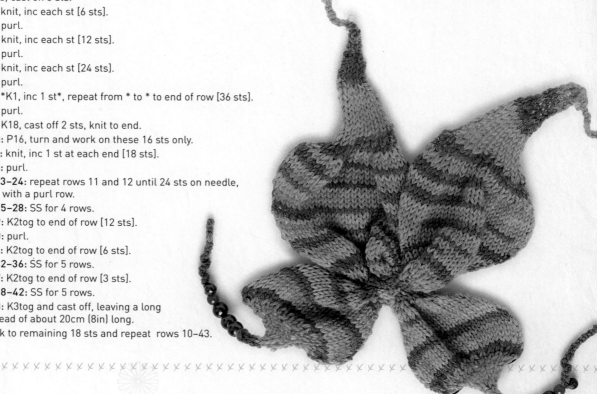

Oberon the Fairy King

With his shock of long, green wavy hair topped
with a golden crown, the King of Fairyland strikes
a handsome figure. He is clothed in the colours
and textures of the forest. His mottled green and
blue breeches are the colour of the lake hidden
deep within the forest where he lives. His brown
jacket trimmed with fur and his sturdy brown boots
are essential as he roams through his kingdom,
sometimes flying high up amongst the foliage with
the aid of his powerful, leaf-like wings.

You will need

All of the items you need to make the fairies in this book are listed on page 8. The specific yarns, needles, threads and embellishments you need to make Oberon are listed below, though you can, of course, use suitable alternatives instead, depending on the style of doll you wish to create and what materials are available to you.

Yarns:

★ mid-brown, flesh-coloured, dark brown and light brown double-knitting yarn (8-ply/light worsted) for body

★ variegated, green unspun fleece for hair and beard

★ mottled green and brown double-knitting yarn (8-ply/light worsted) for breeches

★ eyelash yarn in shades of brown for jacket trim

★ mid-brown double-knitting yarn (8-ply/light worsted) for jacket

★ bright green double-knitting yarn (8-ply/light worsted) for wings

Needles:

★ 3mm (US 3), 7mm (US 11) and 4mm (US 6) knitting needles

Threads:

★ dark brown embroidery thread for eyebrows and eyelashes

For finishing the fairy:

★ Press-stud for fastening jacket; two large, silk leaves for wings; fine, gold-plated copper wire and ten gold beads for crown; small gold-coloured ring for earring; four small tassels for the tops of the boots

Torso and head

Using mid-brown yarn and 3mm (US 3) needles, cast on 24 sts.

rows 1–10: SS, ending with a purl row.

Waist

row 11: K2tog, K5, K2tog, K6, K2tog, K5, K2tog [20 sts].
rows 12–14: SS for 3 rows.
row 15: inc 1 st, K5, inc 1 st, K6, inc 1 st, K5, inc 1 st [24 sts].
rows 16–22: SS for 7 rows.

Shoulders

row 23: K6, inc 2 sts, K8, inc 2 sts, K6 [28 sts].
row 24: purl.
row 25: change to flesh-coloured yarn. K6, K2tog twice, K8, K2tog twice, K6 [24 sts].
row 26: P2tog to end of row [12 sts].
row 27: K2tog, knit to last 2 sts, K2tog [10 sts].

Neck

rows 28–34: SS for 7 rows.

Head

row 35: knit, inc 1 st at each end [12 sts].
row 36: purl, inc 1 st at each end [14 sts].
row 37: K6, inc 2 sts, K6 [16 sts].
row 38: purl.
row 39: inc 3 sts, K3, inc 4 sts, K3, inc 3 sts [26 sts].
row 40: purl.
row 41: knit, inc 1 st at each end [28 sts].
row 42: purl.
row 43: knit, inc 1 st at each end [30 sts].
rows 44–56: SS for 13 rows.
row 57: K2tog to end of row [15 sts].
row 58: purl.
row 59: K1, then K2tog to end of row [8 sts].
row 60: purl.
row 61: K2tog to end of row [4 sts].
row 62: purl and cast off.

Making up

1. Fold the torso in half, right sides together. Using backstitch, sew from the top of the head down to 1cm (½in) from the top of the neck.

2. Sew up the centre back seam from the bottom upwards until you are 1cm (½in) from the start of the neck.
3. Turn right-side out and stuff the top of the head.

Inserting the backbone

1. Take either a piece of dowelling, a roll of cardboard, an unsharpened pencil or a chopstick that is about 1–2cm (½–¾in) shorter than the combined body and head length of the doll.
2. Wrap sticky tape around it, with the sticky side out, so that it is completely covered.
3. Wrap a fine layer of stuffing along the length of the backbone so that all of the sticky surface is covered.
4. Insert the backbone up through the body and into the head of the doll. Once the backbone is in place, add stuffing through the neck opening and into the head. Shape the head with your fingers until it is a nice, even shape. When you are happy with it, mattress stitch the neck closed.
5. Now continue to stuff the body. Shape the shoulders evenly. When you are finished, whip stitch the base of the body closed.

Ears

Make two.

With flesh-coloured yarn and 3mm (US 3) needles, cast on 3 sts, leaving a long tail at each end.

row 1: knit, inc each st [6 sts].

row 2: purl.

row 3: knit, inc 1 st at each end [8 sts].

row 4: purl.

row 5: knit, inc 1 st at each end [10 sts].

row 6: purl and cast off.

Making up the ears

You may find it easier to position the ears once you have created the face.

1. Place both ears in front of you so that one is the mirror image of the other. The longer side is the outer rim of the ear, so have these facing outwards.

2. For both ears, use the left-over tail thread at the bottom of the ear to make small running stitches around the lobe and up the outer rim. Pull the thread firmly so that the ear lobe becomes rounded in shape. Secure with a small stitch, neaten the thread and cut off. Leave the other tail thread and use it to secure the ear to the side of the head. This should make a fairy-like ear, slightly pointed at the top and round at the bottom.

3. Pin the ears to the side of the head, slightly nearer to the back of the head than to the front. Make sure the two ears are level, and align the side of the ear that will be attached to the head with the edge of the nose. Mattress stitch each ear to the head using the spare tail threads.

4. Make a stitch securing the middle of each ear to the head, thus pinning the ears back so they do not stick out. Neaten the threads and cut off the excess.

Arms

Make two.

With flesh-coloured yarn and 3mm (US 3) needles, cast on 3 sts.

row 1: knit, inc each st [6 sts].

row 2: purl.

row 3: knit, inc 1 st at each end [8 sts].

rows 4–6: SS for 3 rows.

row 7: cast on 3 sts, knit to end [11 sts].

row 8: cast on 3 sts, purl to end [14 sts].

row 9: cast off 3 sts, knit to end [11 sts].

row 10: cast off 3 sts, purl to end [8 sts].

row 11: K2tog, knit to last 2 sts, K2tog [6 sts].

rows 12–40: change to mid-brown yarn and SS for 29 rows.

row 41: K2tog to end of row [3 sts].

row 42: purl and cast off.

Making up the arms

1. Fold each arm in half lengthwise, wrong sides together, and mattress stitch from the tip of the fingers to 1cm (½in) below the top of the arm. Do not stuff the arms.

2. Pin each arm in place on the body so that the top of each arm is flush with the shoulder. Make sure the arms are evenly placed, then use mattress stitch to sew them in position around the armhole. Neaten the threads and trim them off.

Face

See pages 9–10 for needlesculpting the face and making the eyes, nose and lips.

Oberon's nose is embroidered from the tip up to the eyes, with the tip of the nose much wider than the bridge. His eyes are coloured using golden brown for the irises and brown on the lids. His straight eyebrows are embroidered on using several strands of brown embroidery thread, and his red lips are cut from dark red felt. On his chin I have attached a few strands of green, unspun fleece using a crochet hook (see below).

Hair

Oberon's hair is made using green, unspun fleece, which I have cut into short lengths of about 10cm (4in) and hooked through the knitting stitches on his scalp using a crochet hook (see page 11). Once you have achieved a dense covering of hair, trim to the required length.

Legs

Make two.
Using dark brown yarn and 3mm (US 3) needles, cast on 3 sts.
row 1: knit, inc each st across row [6 sts].
row 2: purl.
row 3: knit, inc 1 st at each end [8 sts].
row 4: purl.
rows 5–12: repeat rows 3 and 4 until 16 sts on needle, ending with a purl row.
rows 13–16: SS for 4 rows.
row 17: K2tog twice, K8, K2tog twice [12 sts].
row 18: purl.
row 19: K2tog twice, K4, K2 tog twice [8 sts].
rows 20–24: SS for 5 rows.
row 25: inc 1 st, knit to end of row [9 sts].
row 26: inc 1 st, purl to end of row [10 sts].
rows 27–28: repeat rows 25 and 26 [12 sts].
rows 29–36: SS for 8 rows.
rows 37–42: GS for 6 rows.
rows 43–72: change to light brown yarn and SS for 30 rows. Cast off on last row.

Making up the legs

1. Fold the legs, wrong sides together, and mattress stitch from the toe to the top of the leg. Stuff the legs firmly but don't over stuff.
2. Place the legs evenly under the base of the body, making sure the leg seam is at the back. Whip stitch the legs on to the body and neaten and trim the threads.

Finishing the body

Needlesculpt the body and head following the instructions on page 9.

Breeches

Make two.
Using variegated green and blue yarn and 4mm (US 6) needles, cast on 16 sts.
rows 1–5: GS.
rows 6–20: SS for 15 rows, beginning and ending with a purl row.
row 21: knit, inc 1 st at each end [18 sts].
row 22: purl.
row 23: knit, inc 1 st at each end [20 sts].
row 24: purl.
row 25: K8, K2tog twice, K8 [18 sts].
rows 26–34: SS for 9 rows.
row 35: K2tog, knit to last 2 sts, K2tog [16 sts].
row 36: knit.
row 37: K4, K2tog, K4, K2tog, K4 [14 sts].
rows 38–40: GS and cast off on last row.

Making up the breeches

1. Place the two pieces of knitting with right sides together. On each side of the knitting, backstitch down from the waist to the crotch.
2. Unfold the breeches and refold them so that the two seams are now in the middle, one on top of the other (still with right sides together). Backstitch from one leg opening, across the crotch and down to the other leg opening. Neaten the threads and turn right-side out.

Jacket

Back

Make one.
Using eyelash yarn and 4mm (US 6) needles, cast on 18 sts.
rows 1–8: GS.
rows 9–23: change to brown yarn and SS for 15 rows. Cast off on the last row.

Front

Make two.
Using eyelash yarn and 4mm (US 6) needles, cast on 10 sts.
rows 1–8: GS.
rows 9–23: change to brown yarn and SS for 15 rows. Cast off on the last row.

Sleeves

Make two.
Using eyelash yarn and 4mm (US 6) needles, cast on 14 sts.
rows 1–8: GS.
rows 9–22: change to brown yarn and SS for 14 rows. Cast off on the last row.

Making up the jacket

1. Place the jacket back right-side up. Place the two top pieces, side by side, on top of it, right sides down. Backstitch the shoulder seams to about halfway across each front piece.
2. When the shoulders are sewn, unfold the jacket and lay it completely flat, right side down. Position the sleeves, right sides down, so that the centre top of each sleeve aligns with the shoulder seam. Backstitch each sleeve on to the jacket.
3. Fold the jacket inside out and backstitch down one sleeve from the wrist to the armhole seam, then down the side seam of the coat. Repeat on the other side. Turn the jacket right-side out.
4. Sew one half of a press-stud on to either side of the jacket front to fasten.

Wings

With bright green yarn and 4mm (US 6) needles, cast on 3 sts.

row 1: knit, inc each st [6 sts].
row 2: purl.
row 3: knit, inc 1 st at each end [8 sts].
rows 4–22: SS for 19 rows.
row 23: K2, K2tog twice, K2 [6 sts].
rows 24–26: SS for 3 rows.
row 27: k1, k2tog twice, k1 [4]
row 28: purl.
row 29: K2tog and cast off.

Making up the wings

1. Place the wings right sides facing and stitch them together at the base with a 1cm (½in) seam. Wire the wings if necessary (see page 9).
2. Take two large silk leaves, bind them together at the stem and stitch them in place behind the knitted leaves.
3. Sew one half of a press-stud fastening on to the centre front of the knitted leaves, and the other half to the back of the fairy's jacket in the middle. Alternatively, stitch the wings directly on to the fairy.

To finish the fairy

1. Make the crown from fine, gold-plated copper wire. First form the base of the crown by making a circle of wire the correct size to fit on the fairy's head. Twist the ends together to secure.
2. Make each point from a length of wire about 11cm (4¼in) long. Wrap one end of the wire around the base two or three times, then thread on a gold bead and position it centrally so that it sits at the top. Twist the wire to secure the bead, then form the point and attach the other end of the wire to the base. Work your way around the crown, shaping the points by bending them outwards slightly.
3. Thread a small gold-coloured ring through one of the fairy's earlobes.
4. Stitch two small tassels to the top of each boot.

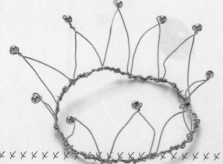

Titania the Fairy Queen

The Queen of Fairyland is a gentle beauty. Her long, brown, wavy hair, pretty green wings and soft furry gown keep her well hidden amongst the leaves and branches of the forest canopy that she inhabits. Her friends are the birds and beasts of the woodland, though her true love is Oberon, with whom she can often be spied walking hand in hand through their beloved kingdom.

You will need

All of the items you need to make the fairies in this book are listed on page 8. The specific yarns, needles, threads and embellishments you need to make Oberon are listed below, though you can, of course, use suitable alternatives instead, depending on the style of doll you wish to create and what materials are available to you.

Yarns:

* Rust-coloured and flesh-coloured double-knitting yarn (8-ply/light worsted) for body
* Brown double-knitting yarn (8-ply/light worsted), knitted up and unravelled, for hair
* Variegated fluffy yarn in browns, reds and purples for skirt
* Gold, sparkly yarn (any weight) for skirt ties
* Light brown yarn (any weight) for berries
* Light green, light DK (5-ply/sport) yarn for leaf collar
* Dark green, light DK (5-ply/sport) yarn for wings

Needles:

* 3mm (US 3), 7mm (US 11) and 4mm (US 6) knitting needles

Threads:

* Brown embroidery thread for eyebrows and eyelashes

For finishing the fairy:

* Gold-plated copper wire and six gold beads for tiara

Torso and head

Using rust-coloured yarn and 3mm (US 3) needles, cast on 24 sts.

rows 1–10: SS, ending with a purl row.

Waist

row 11: K2tog, K5, K2tog, K6, K2tog, K5, K2tog [20 sts].
rows 12–14: SS for 3 rows.
row 15: inc 1 st, K5, inc 1 st, K6, inc 1 st, K5, inc 1 st [24 sts].
rows 16–22: SS for 7 rows.

Shoulders

row 23: change to flesh-coloured yarn and K6, inc 2 sts, K8, inc 2 sts, K6 [28 sts].
row 24: purl.
row 25: K6, K2tog twice, K8, K2tog twice, K6 [24 sts].
row 26: P2tog to end of row [12 sts].
row 27: K2tog, knit to last 2 sts, K2tog [10 sts].

Neck

rows 28–34: SS for 7 rows.

Head

row 35: knit, inc 1 st at each end [12 sts].
row 36: purl, inc 1 st at each end [14 sts].
row 37: K6, inc 2 sts, K6 [16 sts].
row 38: purl.
row 39: inc 3 sts, K3, inc 4 sts, K3, inc 3 sts [26 sts].
row 40: purl.
row 41: knit, inc 1 st at each end [28 sts].
row 42: purl.
row 43: knit, inc 1 st at each end [30 sts].
rows 44–56: SS for 13 rows.
row 57: K2tog to end of row [15 sts].
row 58: purl.
row 59: K1, then K2tog to end of row [8 sts].
row 60: purl.
row 61: K2tog to end of row [4 sts].
row 62: purl and cast off.

Making up

1. Fold the torso in half, right sides together. Using backstitch, sew from the top of the head down to 1cm (½in) from the top of the neck.

2. Sew up the centre back seam from the bottom upwards until you are 1cm (½in) from the start of the neck.
3. Turn right-side out and stuff the top of the head.

Inserting the backbone

1. Take either a piece of dowelling, a roll of cardboard, an unsharpened pencil or a chopstick that is about 1–2cm (½–¾in) shorter than the combined body and head length of the doll.
2. Wrap sticky tape around it, with the sticky side out, so that it is completely covered.
3. Wrap a fine layer of stuffing along the length of the backbone so that all of the sticky surface is covered.
4. Insert the backbone up through the body and into the head of the doll. Once the backbone is in place, add stuffing through the neck opening and into the head. Shape the head with your fingers until it is a nice, even shape. When you are happy with it, mattress stitch the neck closed.
5. Now continue to stuff the body. Shape the shoulders evenly. When you are finished, whip stitch the base of the body closed.

Ears

Make two.

Using flesh-coloured yarn and 3mm (US 3) needles, cast on 3 sts, leaving a long tail at each end.

row 1: knit, inc each st [6 sts].
row 2: purl.
row 3: knit, inc 1 st at each end [8 sts].
row 4: purl.
row 5: knit, inc 1 st at each end [10 sts].
row 6: purl and cast off.

Making up the ears

You may find it easier to position the ears once you have created the face.

1. Place both ears in front of you so that one is the mirror image of the other. The longer side is the outer rim of the ear, so have these facing outwards.

2. For both ears, use the left-over tail thread at the bottom of the ear to make small running stitches around the lobe and up the outer rim. Pull the thread firmly so that the ear lobe becomes rounded in shape. Secure with a small stitch, neaten the thread and cut off. Leave the other tail thread and use it to secure the ear to the side of the head. This should make a fairy-like ear, slightly pointed at the top and round at the bottom.

3. Pin the ears to the side of the head, slightly nearer to the back of the head than to the front. Make sure the two ears are level, and align the side of the ear that will be attached to the head with the edge of the nose. Mattress stitch each ear to the head using the spare tail threads.

4. Make a stitch securing the middle of each ear to the head, thus pinning the ears back so they do not stick out. Neaten the threads and cut off the excess.

Arms

Make two.

With flesh-coloured yarn and 3mm (US 3) needles, cast on 3 sts.

row 1: knit, inc each st [6 sts].
row 2: purl.
row 3: knit, inc 1 st at each end [8 sts].
rows 4–6: SS for 3 rows.
row 7: cast on 3 sts, knit to end [11 sts].
row 8: cast on 3 sts, purl to end [14 sts].

row 9: cast off 3 sts, knit to end [11 sts].
row 10: cast off 3 sts, purl to end [8 sts].
row 11: K2tog, knit to last 2 sts, K2tog [6 sts].
rows 12–40: SS for 29 rows.
row 41: K2tog to end of row [3 sts].
row 42: purl and cast off.

Making up the arms

1. Fold each arm in half lengthwise, wrong sides together, and mattress stitch from the tip of the fingers to 1cm (½in) below the top of the arm. Do not stuff the arms.

2. Pin each arm in place on the body so that the top of each arm is flush with the shoulder. Make sure the arms are evenly placed, then use mattress stitch to sew them in position around the armhole. Neaten the threads and trim them off.

Legs

Make two.
Using flesh-coloured yarn and 3mm (US 3) needles, cast on 3 sts.
row 1: knit, inc in each st [6 sts].
row 2: purl.
row 3: knit, inc in each st [12 sts].
rows 4–8: SS for 5 rows.
row 9: K2tog to end of row [6 sts].
row 10 onwards: SS until leg measure 23cm (9in) from the tip of the toe and cast off.

Making up the legs

1. Fold the legs, wrong sides together, and mattress stitch from the toe to the top of the leg. Do not stuff the female fairy legs.
2. Place the legs evenly under the base of the body, making sure the leg seam is at the back. Whip stitch the legs on to the body and neaten and trim the threads.

Finishing the body

Needlesculpt the body and head following the instructions on page 9.

Face

See pages 9–10 for needlesculpting the face and making the eyes, nose and lips.

I have given Titania a sweet button nose by embroidering just the tip using a row of vertical straight stitches. Her irises are coloured blue and her eyelids brown. I have embroidered on her thin eyebrows using a single stitch for each, and two or three eyelashes at the outer edge of each eye. Titania's rosebud lips are cut from deep red felt. I have added no colouring to her face, leaving it pale and natural.

Hair

See the general instructions on page 11. Here I have used a brown yarn, which I knitted up, left for a few days and then unravelled, resulting in a tight wave that suits Titania's long, curly hair perfectly.

1. Wind the yarn around a large book to obtain the length of hair you want, and cut along one edge.
2. Take each strand in turn, fold it in half and hook it through a single knitted stitch on the fairy's scalp with a crochet hook.
3. Once the head is covered in a good, thick layer of hair, trim the hair to the correct length if desired.
4. As a final touch, I scooped up the sides of Titania's hair and held it in place with a string of gold beads.

Skirt

Using 7mm (US 11) needles and fluffy yarn, cast on 50 sts.
rows 1–15: GS.
row 16: K2tog to end of row [25 sts].
row 17: knit.
row 18: K2tog six times, K1, K2tog six times [13 sts].
rows 19–20: GS and cast off on last row.

Making up the skirt

1. Crochet 2 chains using gold, sparkly yarn, each 15cm (6in) long, or knit 2 chains using knit 1 st, turn, knit 1 st. Alternatively, use lengths of fine ribbon.
2. Attach a chain to either side of the waist. Wrap the skirt around the fairy and tie it in place.

Berries

Make three or four.
Using light brown yarn and 3mm (US 3) needles, cast on 3 sts.
row 1: knit, inc each st [6 sts].
row 2: purl.
rows 3–4: repeat rows 1 and 2 [12 sts].
row 5: K2tog to end of row [6 sts].
row 6: purl.
rows 7–8: repeat rows 5 and 6, casting off on last row.

Making up the berries

1. Mattress stitch up the centre seam of each berry, right-side out. Add a little stuffing as you go until you have formed a tiny ball. Stitch the berry closed.
2. Sew a piece of yarn, about 4cm (1½in) long, through the top of each berry and attach the berries to one of the skirt cords at the waist.

Leaf collar

Make three.
Using silky, light green light DK (5-ply/sport) yarn and 3mm (US 3) needles, cast on 2 sts.
row 1: knit, inc each st [4 sts].
row 2: purl.
rows 3–4: repeat rows 1 and 2 until 8 sts on needle, ending with a purl row.
rows 5–8: SS for 4 rows.
row 9: K2tog to end of row [4 sts].
row 10: P2tog twice [2 sts].
row 11: knit and cast off.

Making up the collar

Stitch the three leaves to the bodice top – one along the front and one over each shoulder.

Wings

Make four.
Using light DK (5-ply/sport) silky, dark green yarn and 3mm (US 3) needles, cast on 2 sts.
row 1: knit, inc 1 st at start and end of row [4 sts].
row 2: purl.
rows 3–12: repeat rows 1 and 2 until 14 sts on needle, ending with a purl row.
rows 13–16: SS for 4 rows.
row 17: K2tog to end of row [7 sts].
row 18: purl.
row 19: K2tog, K3, K2tog [5 sts].
row 20: P2tog, P1, P2tog [3 sts].
row 21: knit and cast off.

Making up the wings

1. Place two wing pieces with right sides together and stitch them together at the base with a 1cm (½in) seam. Repeat for the other two wings.

2. Open out each pair of wings and place one on top of the other, right sides together. Stitch them together with a 2cm (¾in) seam (1cm/½in either side of the centre seam).

3. Unfold the wings and sew on one half of a press-stud fastening on the centre front (where the four wings meet). Sew the corresponding half on to the back of the fairy, in the middle. Alternatively, stitch the wings straight on to the fairy's back.

To finish the fairy

1. Make the tiara from fine, gold-plated copper wire, 45–50cm (18–20in) long. Thread a gold bead on to the wire, about 15cm (6in) from one end, and bend the ends down. Hold the bead firmly and twist the two ends of wire together to make a stem 2–3cm (about 1in) long.

2. Continue along the wire, making five more twisted stems with a gold bead at the top of each one, leaving about 1cm (½in) between them.

3. Bend the wire on each side of the tiara in two and twist together to form a length of about 5cm (2in).

Index

For a complete list of all our books see

www.searchpress.com

Knitted Aliens

Knitted Bears
Val Pierce

Knitted Pirates, Princesses, Witches, Wizards & Fairies
with outfits & accessories

RSN Essential Stitch Guides
JACQUI MCDONALD
Crewelwork
SEARCH PRESS

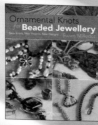
Ornamental Knots for Beaded Jewellery
Suzen Millodot

Tiaras & Hairpins
Michelle Bungay

Polymer Clay Beaded JEWELLERY
35 Beautiful Designs

STITCH CLOTH PAPER & PAINT
Mixed Media Ideas & Inspiration

Knitted Cakes
Susan Penny

FROM PRINT TO STITCH

HOW TO MAKE Friendship Bracelets
Veronique Follet

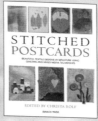
STITCHED POSTCARDS
EDITED BY CHRISTA ROLF
SEARCH PRESS

Beaded Felt Jewellery
Helen Birmingham

Simple Recipes for Stylish Jewellery
Over 80 Projects

Tasty Trinkets
Charlotte Stowell

FIGURE POSES FOR FASHION ILLUSTRATORS

Babes in the Wool

Fabulous Bags to Stitch & Make
Jenny Rolfe

Stylish Sewing

Sew Scandinavian

FOLLOW US ON:

twitter

www.twitter.com/searchpress

facebook

Search Press Art and Craft Books

To request a free catalogue, go to http://www.searchpress.com/requestcat.asp